I0605987
To
From
Date

3-Minute Devotions for Girls

Consider the Lilies

3-Minute Devotions for Girls

Consider the Lilies

MariLee Parrish

Print ISBN 979-8-89151-087-6

Published by Barbour Publishing, Inc., 1810 Barbour Drive, Uhrichsville, Ohio 44683, www.barbourbooks.com

Our mission is to inspire the world with the life-changing message of the Bible.

Printed in China.
002431 0425 HA

Take a Few Moments to Consider the Lilies. . .

"Can all your worries add a single moment to your life? And if worry can't accomplish a little thing like that, what's the use of worrying over bigger things? Look at the lilies and how they grow. They don't work or make their clothing, yet Solomon in all his glory was not dressed as beautifully as they are. And if God cares so wonderfully for flowers that are here today and thrown into the fire tomorrow, he will certainly care for you. Why do you have so little faith?"

Luke 12:25–28 NLT

You matter. And you have a purpose. And God cares wonderfully for you. Not because of anything you've done or could ever do on your own but simply because you're His kid. His beloved daughter. God's chosen one, holy and blameless because of Jesus. Set free and empowered with God's Spirit to bring light to a dark world.

In this book, we'll focus on who God is, who God says you are, and why that even matters, all while taking hold of truth even in times of doubt. Every devotion will tell you more about who God is and who you are *because* of Him.

Ask God to show Himself to you. He really loves doing that!

With love and great hope,
MariLee

Unchanging, Everlasting God

"I, even I, am the Lord. There is no one who saves except Me. . . . I am God and always will be. No one is able to take anything out of My hand. I do something, and who can change it?"
Isaiah 43:11, 13

We live in a world where both kids and grown-ups are addicted to their screens, and so many messages come at us every day that it's hard to relate to the real world. Lots of things we see and hear are even fake, making it hard to know what's true, real, and good. But God wants you to know and live in the truth that *He* is real and good and that *you* matter to Him. Throughout these devotions, we'll ask God to reveal what's fake and uncover lies we might be believing. We'll also ask Him to teach us His truth. Because the truth of God never changes, the truth of who you are and how much you matter never changes.

God, please show Yourself and Your truth to me. I'm so thankful that I matter to You.

The Truth

The Lord, Who makes you, bought you and saves you, and the One Who put you together before you were born, says, "I am the Lord, Who made all things. I alone spread out the heavens, and I alone spread out the earth."

Isaiah 44:24

We can learn lots of truth from Isaiah 44:24:

- God made you.
- He bought you with His blood on the cross and saved you, so you now belong to Him.
- He knew you before you were even born.
- God made all things, including heaven and earth.

The Maker of the universe made you and knows everything about you. You matter so much to Him that He paid for your life and all your sins on a cross. Through Jesus, you belong to God and have His Spirit alive inside you.

Jesus, thank You for taking away all my sins and showing me how much I matter to You. I choose to follow You. Thank You that Your Holy Spirit is alive and at work in my heart.

Following God

"Remember the things of long ago.
For I am God, and there is no other.
I am God, and there is no one like Me."
ISAIAH 46:9

As a growing follower of Jesus, you need to know some important, true things. These truths will help you understand how you can matter so much to God! Our God is the one true God, and He exists as God the Father, Jesus, and the Holy Spirit. The Bible says Jesus is the image of the invisible God. That means Jesus is God in a physical body (Colossians 1:15). We pray to God through the power of the Holy Spirit, who comes alive inside us when we choose to follow Jesus. That's a lot of information to take in! It helps to close your eyes and try to picture all this in your head. Ask Jesus to help you understand these truths.

Jesus, I'm excited to be Your follower. I want to learn everything I can about You and why I matter so much to You! Please help me understand.

Jesus Died for You

After they had made fun of Him, they took the coat off and put His own clothes on Him. Then they led Him away to be nailed to a cross.
MATTHEW 27:31

God is holy and perfect in all His ways. We are not. We sin. We mess up. We've all made lots of mistakes. We can't understand everything about God or His ways, but we do know we can't get to God if we aren't perfect. *What?* you say. But that's why Jesus came! He's the only person who has never sinned, so He took our place and took on all our sins and washed them away in His blood. That's how much you matter to God! Jesus' death on the cross was the only way for us to be with God. Let's learn more about what Jesus did for us over the next few days.

Jesus, I believe You took all the punishment for my sins. I don't understand everything about that, but I'm sorry You went through such suffering for me. You must really love me a lot!

Free Will

Christ never sinned but God put our sin on Him. Then we are made right with God because of what Christ has done for us.
2 Corinthians 5:21

God made us and loves us so much. But He made each of us with the ability to make our own choices because He didn't want to create robots who were programmed to do what He said. This is called "free will." He wants each of us to choose to love Him and follow Him. We can choose to live in our sin and selfishness, forever separated from God. Or we can choose to accept the righteousness (that big word means perfectness) of Jesus and be with God for eternity. Jesus died to take our sins so that when God looks at us, He sees the perfect sacrifice Jesus made for us instead. Jesus came and died so that we can be made perfect before God. It was the only way.

Wow. You see me as perfect because of Jesus? That is so amazing, God! I'm so thankful!

The Choice to Follow Jesus

But you are not doing what your sinful old selves want you to do. You are doing what the Holy Spirit tells you to do, if you have God's Spirit living in you. No one belongs to Christ if he does not have Christ's Spirit in him.

ROMANS 8:9

God wants you to know that Jesus Christ can live in you! The same power that raised Jesus from the grave is what God offers all of us who believe. Will you accept His gift? He gave His life to offer you a relationship with God. Why? Because you matter to Him and He loves you so very much! All you have to do is believe and invite Him to be your Lord (the boss of your life) and Savior (understanding that He paid the price for your sins and gives you eternal life with God). Talk to a parent or a trusted grown-up about your choice to follow Jesus.

Thank You for coming for me, Jesus.
I invite You into my life. Be the boss of my life.

Your Heart Matters to Jesus

"The Spirit of the Lord is on Me. He has put His hand on Me to preach the Good News to poor people. He has sent Me to heal those with a sad heart. He has sent Me to tell those who are being held that they can go free. He has sent Me to make the blind to see and to free those who are held because of trouble."

Luke 4:18

When Jesus first started His ministry on earth, He stood in front of people and told them why He had come. He came for everyone, and that includes you. Jesus didn't just mean He came to bring good news to people who have no money (although He came for them too); He also came for people who are needy and feel powerless. Children are often needy and have little power over their lives. Jesus was talking about you here. He cares about your heart and all your feelings.

Jesus, thank You for coming for me and loving me so much!

Who You Really Are, Part 1

God's Word is living and powerful. . . . It tells what the heart is thinking about and what it wants to do.

Hebrews 4:12

Because of what Jesus has done for you, all these things below are true. These truths will help you know how much you matter to God! Say these out loud:

- I am free and clean in the blood of Christ (Galatians 5:1; 1 John 1:7; Galatians 5:1).
- God has rescued me from darkness and brought me into His kingdom (Colossians 1:13).
- I have direct access to God (Ephesians 2:18).
- I am a precious child of the Father (Isaiah 43:6–7; John 1:12; Galatians 3:26).
- I am a friend of Christ's (John 15:15).
- Nothing can separate me from God's love (Romans 8:38–39).
- God is for me, not against me (Romans 8:31).

Copy this list and post it where you can see it daily. Stay tuned for more of these truths tomorrow!

God, thank You for telling me the truth about who I am.

Who You Really Are, Part 2

"Make them holy for Yourself by the truth. Your Word is truth."
John 17:17

All God's words are true, and it matters so much to Him that you know and believe His truth. Here's more about who God says you are! Say these out loud:

- God sees me as beautiful, and I am wonderfully made (Psalm 139:14; Ecclesiastes 3:11).
- God sings over me (Zephaniah 3:17).
- God delights in me (Psalm 149:4).
- I am God's temple (1 Corinthians 3:16).
- I am the light of the world (Matthew 5:14).
- I am chosen by God (Colossians 3:12).
- God will meet all my needs (Philippians 4:19).
- I am dearly loved (John 3:16; Jeremiah 31:3).
- I am a child of the King. I am royalty. . .a princess (John 1:12; 1 Timothy 6:15)!

Your Word is clear about how much I matter to You, God. Thanks for making me feel so special! Help me believe everything You say and to live like I believe it.

Repent and Believe

At one time you were strangers to God and your minds were at war with Him. Your thoughts and actions were wrong. But Christ has brought you back to God by His death on the cross. In this way, Christ can bring you to God, holy and pure and without blame.

Colossians 1:21–22

One of the enemy's goals is to attack your identity in Christ—these truths we've been learning about—so you won't know who you really are and the power you have because of Christ living in you. God wants you to stand against these lies from the enemy that cause you to doubt. It's important to repent when you catch yourself believing any of these lies. That means you ask God to forgive you and you turn back toward Him. God wants you to believe and walk in His truth. You are who He says you are, and that's the whole truth.

Dear God, help me walk in the truth of who You say I am.

God Lives in You

You are also being put together as a part of this building because God lives in you by His Spirit.
Ephesians 2:22

As in Ephesians 2:22, the Bible uses lots of word pictures to help us understand certain ideas. As God's children, we're part of His family together with all other Christ followers. We're also the body of Christ, the church. When Jesus returned to heaven, He sent His Spirit to live in our hearts, and we became His hands and feet here on earth. Jesus gets His physical work done here by using us. It matters what you do, how you feel, and what you believe because you are God's representative. When people see you, they're experiencing God through you. Ask Him to fill you up with His love and joy so others can see how much they matter to God.

God, thank You that Your Spirit is alive in me. Please fill me up with love and joy so I can love others like You do.

Kids Are Special

At that time Jesus said, "Thank You, Father, Lord of heaven and earth, because You hid these things from the wise and from those who have much learning. You have shown them to little children."

MATTHEW 11:25

We've been learning a lot about who God is and who God says you are. Now, some of these truths might be a little confusing. But that's because God is *so big* that we can't possibly understand everything about Him. But here's the amazing thing: whenever you have a question about Jesus, just ask Him! You are so special to Jesus. He wants to tell you things about Himself some adults can't even understand. Kids can often sense things grown-ups can't. They also innocently tell the truth, and they love with all their hearts. Jesus loves kids, and He thinks they matter a lot. He wants grown-ups to believe in Him the way kids do.

Jesus, I'm so thankful that You want me to know who You are. Please work in my heart as I learn more about You. Help me trust You.

Set Apart

I write to God's church in the city of Corinth. I write to those who belong to Christ Jesus and to those who are set apart by Him and made holy. I write to all the Christians everywhere who call on the name of Jesus Christ. He is our Lord and their Lord also.

1 Corinthians 1:2

You are really quite special! Did you know that? God says you're set apart and made holy because of what Jesus did for you. God is always looking at you with love. Have you ever caught a parent looking at you when they think you're asleep? Parents have a certain love-look on their faces only for their children. You have a special place in God's heart, too, and He is the perfect parent. He's always looking at you with a special look of love. Even though this world He made has billions of people in it, you are still special to Him.

God, I don't understand how I could possibly be special to You, but I believe it's true! Thanks for loving me.

Two Families

Even before the world was made, God chose us for Himself because of His love. He planned that we should be holy and without blame as He sees us.

EPHESIANS 1:4

Check out the Message paraphrase of Ephesians 1:4–5: "Long before he laid down earth's foundations, he had us in mind, had settled on us as the focus of his love, to be made whole and holy by his love. Long, long ago he decided to adopt us into his family through Jesus Christ. (What pleasure he took in planning this!)" Adopted kids are chosen specifically by their parents, and that's exactly what God has done for you! Yes, God placed you in a family on earth to care for and love you (whether you were born into your family or adopted. . .and that was part of His plan), but the big-picture story of your life is that God adopted you into His family—forever.

God, I'm so thankful that I'm part of two families! Thank You for choosing me.

Your Inheritance

We will receive the great things that we have been promised. They are being kept safe in heaven for us. They are pure and will not pass away. They will never be lost. You are being kept by the power of God because you put your trust in Him and you will be saved from the punishment of sin at the end of the world.

1 Peter 1:4–5

An inheritance is something that eventually belongs to you because you were born into a certain family. Royal families with lots of wealth have riches that have been passed down from generation to generation. God promises that you will receive an inheritance too. Because of Jesus, a great inheritance is reserved for you in heaven. We will all get to share in everything good that God has created. First Peter 1:6 sums it up for us: "With this hope you can be happy even if you need to have sorrow and all kinds of tests for awhile."

My hope is in You, God. Thank You for sharing Your goodness with me.

Tough Days

I receive joy when I am weak. I receive joy when people talk against me and make it hard for me and try to hurt me and make trouble for me. I receive joy when all these things come to me because of Christ. For when I am weak, then I am strong.

2 Corinthians 12:10

Have you ever had a bad day? What made it bad? How did you get through it? It's true—life on this planet can be hard some days. But God promises to be with you, and He gives you what you need to get through any hard thing that comes your way. Over the next few days, we'll talk about what God provides to help you not only get through every hard situation but, as 2 Corinthians 12:10 says, to also help you receive joy. He gives you His strength and His armor.

God, thank You for providing for me in every way! When I feel weak, You fill me with Your strength.

Be Strong

Be strong with the Lord's strength.
Put on the things God gives you to fight with.
Then you will not fall into the traps of the devil.
Ephesians 6:10–11

The Bible tells us we have an enemy. He's known as the father of lies (John 8:44), the accuser who makes us feel bad about ourselves (Revelation 12:10), and the ruler of darkness (Ephesians 6:12). But here's the really important thing you need to know: because of Jesus, Satan doesn't have any power over you (Colossians 2:15)! Even though the enemy knows he's been defeated, he's still trying his best to get into your head and discourage you so much that you won't be able to live for Jesus. That's why Jesus wants you to stay alert and put on your armor. Read Ephesians 6:10–18 as we get ready to learn more about our armor. Because you matter so much, God has given you weapons to protect you from the enemy.

Lord, thank You for giving me armor to protect myself against my enemy.

The Belt of Truth

Because of this, put on all the things God gives you to fight with. Then you will be able to stand in that sinful day. When it is all over, you will still be standing. So stand up and do not be moved. Wear a belt of truth around your body.

EPHESIANS 6:13–14

The first piece of armor God gives you is called the "belt of truth." A soldier in battle during Bible times wore a belt to secure all the other pieces of his armor. The belt of truth helps keep everything in the right place. When you're firmly grounded in the truth from God's Word, you can stand strong, and you won't believe the enemy's lies about who you are or who God is. Can you picture yourself putting on God's armor? Start with the belt of truth.

God, please help me know the truth of who I am and who You are so I can stand firm against the enemy's lies.

The Breastplate of Righteousness

Wear a piece of iron over your chest which is being right with God.
EPHESIANS 6:14

A breastplate was a strong piece of iron that soldiers wore over their chests to protect their hearts and other major organs. First Corinthians 1:30 (NLT) tells us that "Christ made us right with God; he made us pure and holy, and he freed us from sin." Righteousness means being right with God. Because of Jesus, nothing can change the fact that God sees us as pure and holy. Jesus took all the punishment for our mistakes. We are not held eternally responsible for sin. So that means we are right with God, or righteous. When you remind yourself of this truth every day, you're protecting your heart from lies and discouragement. You don't have to work hard to take your sins away. That battle has been won by Jesus. Picture yourself putting on the breastplate to protect your heart.

Jesus, thank You for making me righteous before God. Protect my heart from sin and discouragement.

The Shoes of Peace

Wear shoes on your feet which are the Good News of peace.
Ephesians 6:15

Have you ever seen a pair of athletic shoes with spikes on them? These are used to help athletes get a firm grip on the track or field. Soldiers in Bible times would often have spikes on their shoes to keep their feet firmly planted on the ground. God tells us this is an important piece of armor to wear. Can you guess why? The shoes of peace can help you walk in the ways of Jesus and protect you from going down a dangerous path. Jesus came to show you the way to peace with God. He wants you to live in that peace and share it with others. As you walk toward others in love and peace, ask Jesus to give you courage to share His peace with others. Picture yourself putting on the shoes of peace.

Jesus, thank You for Your great gift of peace.
Help me walk in Your ways.

The Shield of Faith

Most important of all, you need a covering of faith in front of you. This is to put out the fire-arrows of the devil.

Ephesians 6:16

The shield of faith protects you from enemy arrows. In Bible times, a soldier had a large shield big enough to hide his whole body behind. It was made of leather and iron. The soldiers soaked their shields in water before a battle, and this put out the arrows the enemy lit on fire and sent their way. As followers of Jesus, we're still in a battle like this. Our enemy likes to throw fiery arrows at us to try to pierce our hearts and get us to believe his lies. Our shield of faith reminds us of who we are in Christ and puts out those fiery darts. Picture yourself holding up your shield of faith.

Lord, as I hold up my shield of faith, thank You for reminding me of Your truth and great love for me. Thank You for Your protection.

The Helmet of Salvation

The covering for your head is that you have been saved from the punishment of sin.

EPHESIANS 6:17

The helmet of salvation protects your head and your mind. As you grow up and go out into this world, you'll have to fight against a lot of messages and lies you may be tempted to believe. But the truth is you are saved from the punishment of sin, you have God's own Spirit and power alive inside you, and you are set apart by God as His beloved daughter. That's the truth you need to wear on your head every single day of your whole entire life. As you picture yourself putting on the helmet of salvation, ask God to help you believe His truth and think His thoughts. Ask Him to protect your mind and keep it pure.

Thank You for my salvation, Lord. I know it cost You everything. Please protect my mind as I put on my helmet of salvation every day.

The Sword of the Spirit

Take the sword of the Spirit which is the Word of God.
EPHESIANS 6:17

The sword of the Spirit—God's Word—is your weapon to attack the enemy and defend yourself against attack. Second Timothy 3:16–17 (NIV) tells us more about this: "All Scripture is God-breathed and is useful for teaching, rebuking, correcting and training in righteousness, so that the servant of God may be thoroughly equipped for every good work." A soldier without a sword won't be able to do very much to win the battle. You need truth from God's Word to effectively defeat the enemy, so it's a really important piece of your spiritual equipment. This is how Jesus defeated Satan in Matthew 4:1–11. As you picture yourself holding your sword, ask God to help you understand and remember His words so you can use them well against your enemy.

Thank You, Lord, for giving me Your armor of protection. Please show me how to use this armor well.

Wear God's Armor Every Day

You must pray at all times as the Holy Spirit leads you to pray. Pray for the things that are needed. You must watch and keep on praying. Remember to pray for all Christians.
Ephesians 6:18

Why is praying and putting on your spiritual armor every day so important? Because you matter to God, and He wants to protect you. The Message paraphrase of the Bible helps us understand a bit more:

> *Be prepared. You're up against far more than you can handle on your own. Take all the help you can get, every weapon God has issued, so that when it's all over but the shouting you'll still be on your feet. Truth, righteousness, peace, faith, and salvation are more than words. Learn how to apply them. You'll need them throughout your life. God's Word is an indispensable weapon. . . . Pray for your brothers and sisters. Keep your eyes open. Keep each other's spirits up so that no one falls behind or drops out.*
> Ephesians 6:13–18

Lord, please remind me of Your truth
as I put on Your armor every day.

Carried by Jesus

The Lord *is my strength and my shield; my heart trusts in him, and he helps me. My heart leaps for joy, and with my song I praise him. The* Lord *is the strength of his people, a fortress of salvation for his anointed one. Save your people and bless your inheritance; be their shepherd and carry them forever.*

Psalm 28:7–9 niv

When God helps, He turns darkness and stress and sadness into joy and singing and thanksgiving! You matter to God, and He is careful with you. He leads you like a gentle shepherd carries his sheep. When you allow Him to help you, miraculous things happen. He knows exactly what you need and how to get you from one step to the next. Can you picture yourself being carried in the arms of Jesus? How does this make you feel?

God, I'm so thankful that You want to help me. I feel so safe when You carry me in Your arms.

Christ in You

I have been put up on the cross to die with Christ. I no longer live. Christ lives in me. The life I now live in this body, I live by putting my trust in the Son of God. He was the One Who loved me and gave Himself for me.

GALATIANS 2:20

Everyone needs this daily reminder: you matter so much to Jesus that He gave His life for you on the cross. The Bible tells us that we were with Jesus on that cross. He died for our sins, and then He rose from the grave showing that He had all power in heaven and earth—even power over death. His Spirit is still alive in us, and we live out His life every day. We are the instruments He uses to do His work on earth. Whenever you feel discouraged, remember that Jesus is alive in you!

Jesus, please help me live my life for You, knowing that You're alive and at work in me. I matter because You say I do.

Caterpillars and Butterflies

For if a man belongs to Christ, he is a new person.
The old life is gone. New life has begun.
2 Corinthians 5:17

Have you ever watched a caterpillar become a butterfly? Ask a parent to help you find a video of this miraculous metamorphosis. A caterpillar has to stop eating, hang upside down, and spin itself into a chrysalis where the metamorphosis occurs before it can become a butterfly. After all that hard work, it becomes a new creation that can fly! The caterpillar is gone, and a beautiful butterfly is here. When you choose to follow Jesus, His Spirit transforms you into a new creation. The great thing is you don't have to work hard like a caterpillar to make this happen. Jesus does this miraculous work in you. The old, selfish you is gone—and you are free to fly!

Jesus, I want to be a new creation in You.
Please do this miraculous work in me and
allow my heart to soar as I follow You.

Marked by God

The truth is the Good News. When you heard the truth, you put your trust in Christ. Then God marked you by giving you His Holy Spirit as a promise.

Ephesians 1:13

When you put your trust in Christ, God marked you as His very own. How did He do this? He sent His Holy Spirit to live inside you. Isn't that amazing? The very Spirit of God is alive in you! What do you think that means? Talk about this with a parent. The Holy Spirit is able to comfort you, teach you, lead you, speak to you, give you good advice, help you think good thoughts, and remember God's words. This is why Jesus said it was better for Him to leave so the Holy Spirit could come (John 16:7)! Jesus was one man who couldn't be everywhere at once. But His Spirit can be in all of us, His children, at the same time!

Jesus, thank You for sending Your Spirit to live inside my heart. I'm so happy to have this miraculous gift!

Loving God and Others

For the love of Christ puts us into action. We are sure that Christ died for everyone. So, because of that, everyone has a part in His death. Christ died for everyone so that they would live for Him. They should not live to please themselves but for Christ Who died on a cross and was raised from the dead for them.

2 Corinthians 5:14–15

Now that we know how much we matter to God and how much He loves us, we can do something about it! Jesus died for us so we would live for Him, and we do this by loving God and loving others. The Bible tells us loving Him and loving others sums up and covers everything God wants us to do. The amazing thing is that God will help you! His Spirit will remind you who you are and show you how to love God and others.

Lord, help me listen for Your Spirit so I can learn to love You and others well.

Sharing God's Love

All this comes from God. He is the One Who brought us to Himself when we hated Him. He did this through Christ. Then He gave us the work of bringing others to Him. God was in Christ. He was working through Christ to bring the whole world back to Himself. God no longer held men's sins against them. And He gave us the work of telling and showing men this.

2 Corinthians 5:18–19

Many of the people who wanted Jesus nailed to the cross hated Him, and many people still hate Him today. Some people just don't believe He's real or that the miracle of the cross ever happened. Some people blame God for other people being mean to them. But Jesus died for those people too. As His children, it's our job to share His love with others. Throughout your lifetime, ask God to help you show others who He really is. God is love.

Lord, I pray for people who don't know how much You love them. Help me show them the truth about who You are.

You're Important

Let no one show little respect for you because you are young. Show other Christians how to live by your life. They should be able to follow you in the way you talk and in what you do. Show them how to live in faith and in love and in holy living.

1 Timothy 4:12

You are important to God. Jesus has always loved children, and He has a special respect for them. All through this book, you'll be reminded again and again that the Spirit of God is alive in you! The same Spirit lives in each one of us—from children who've recently accepted Christ to believers who've walked with Him for a lifetime. Christ in you makes all the difference! He gives you the power to be an example to others. As a young girl, you can inspire and encourage anyone God puts in your life, no matter how old or young they are.

God, thank You for reminding me that I'm important. Please help me be a good example for everyone around me, both young and old.

No More Darkness

God took us out of a life of darkness. He has put us in the holy nation of His much-loved Son.
COLOSSIANS 1:13

The life of Jesus brought light to a very dark world, and His life still brings light to all of us. God's Word says the darkness can never put out the light (John 1:5). That's a promise. Sometimes this world can still seem dark and sad, but remember that we have dual citizenship in heaven. When things seem dark and gloomy here on earth, remember that our forever home is with Jesus. Things that happen here can seem big and bad, but earthly problems will pass away. The light of Jesus lasts forever. Ask Him to light up anything that seems dark to you and to help you bring His powerful light into a dark world.

God, thank You for Your promise that the darkness can never blow out the light. Please fill me with Your light so I can make a difference in a dark world.

The Power Inside You

My children, you are a part of God's family. You have stood against these false preachers and had power over them. You had power over them because the One Who lives in you is stronger than the one who is in the world.

1 John 4:4

The King James Version of the Bible says 1 John 4:4 this way: "Greater is he that is in you, than he that is in the world." This is a powerful verse that's great to remember and say out loud whenever you're afraid. Take a minute right now to write this verse on a sticky note, and then ask the Holy Spirit to help you memorize it. With God's power alive and at work in you, you have nothing to be afraid of. Thank God that He is with you always.

Thanks for being with me all the time, Jesus.
And for caring about the fact that I'm young.
You've given me everything I need to live for You,
including things to remember when I'm afraid.

Which Way Will You Run?

Turn away from the sinful things young people want to do. Go after what is right. Have a desire for faith and love and peace. Do this with those who pray to God from a clean heart. Let me say it again. Have nothing to do with foolish talk and those who want to argue. It can only lead to trouble.

2 Timothy 2:22–23

Paul was a follower of Jesus who wrote a bunch of the New Testament books in the Bible, and he wrote two letters to Timothy to encourage the young minister not to give up. Paul gave Timothy some good advice that God wants us to know today. God wants to help you run away from tempting situations and silly disagreements and run after faith, love, and peace instead. Talk with your family about ways you can do this.

Jesus, please help me run away from sin and silly arguments and run toward faith, love, and peace instead.

Much More

God is able to do much more than we ask
or think through His power working in us.
Ephesians 3:20

God can do way more than we think He can. I mean, after all, He created our brains! He can speak to us and show us things in many different ways. Take a minute right now to think about all the ways God is speaking to you at this very moment: through His Word, through His creation, through music, maybe through the love of a parent or a friend. What other ways is God speaking to you? Being thankful can open our hearts to hearing from God in new ways. What are you thankful for? Can you make a list of ten things you're thankful for? What about fifty things?

God, I am so thankful that You can do much more than anything I could ever imagine. I accept and believe that You can do anything. Open my heart and mind to hearing from You in new ways.

Miracles

Jesus Christ is the same yesterday
and today and forever.
HEBREWS 13:8

God's Word tells us He is the same yesterday, today, and forever. That means God's miracles you've heard about from the Bible are still possible today. He can do again anything He's done before. What miracles do you remember hearing about from the Bible? Can you list some of them? God parted the Red Sea right down the middle so His people could escape from Egypt. Jesus changed water into wine and healed many sick people. He also made enough food for thousands of people to eat out of five loaves of bread and two fish. What else do you remember? Do you believe God can still work those kinds of miracles today? Of course He can! Ask God to help your faith grow.

God, I'm happy to know that You never change. You are still all-powerful and able to do anything. Thank You for Your miracles. Open my mind and heart to believe in them still.

Gifts and Miracles

"O Lord, You have great power, shining-greatness and strength. Yes, everything in heaven and on earth belongs to You. You are the King, O Lord. And You are honored as head over all. Both riches and honor come from You. You rule over all. Power and strength are in Your hand. The power is in Your hand to make great and to give strength to all."

1 Chronicles 29:11–12

James 1:17 (NLT) tells us, "Whatever is good and perfect is a gift coming down to us from God our Father, who created all the lights in the heavens. He never changes." The Lord is the God of the Old and New Testaments. He was powerful then, and He's powerful today. He never changes. He's still capable of all the miracles He's done in the past—and more. Your life matters to God, and every good thing you have is a gift from Him.

Lord, thank You for the great gifts You've given me. You are my God, the God of miracles.

Radiant Light

All of us, with no covering on our faces, show the shining-greatness of the Lord as in a mirror. All the time we are being changed to look like Him, with more and more of His shining-greatness. This change is from the Lord Who is the Spirit.

2 Corinthians 3:18

Many times in the Bible, we're reminded that we're the light of the world. Where does that inner light come from? It comes from God Himself, from spending time in His presence. When you spend much time in the sun, your skin can change color (and sometimes your skin even gets burned!). When you spend time with Jesus, He lights up everything about you, and you matter because you bring God's light to a dark world. Psalm 34:5 (NIV) says, "Those who look to him are radiant; their faces are never covered with shame."

Jesus, remind me that I'm Your light. Continue to change me to look more like You. Let me radiate the light of Your love.

Best Friends

"I do not call you servants that I own anymore. A servant does not know what his owner is doing. I call you friends, because I have told you everything I have heard from My Father."
JOHN 15:15

Do you have a really good friend? A best friend? What makes your friendship special? Good friends know it's important to treat each other with kindness, love, and respect. They spend time together, and they honor each other. Honoring a friend means you think the very best of that person and you put them first instead of being selfish. Jesus calls you His friend. Isn't that awesome? And He wants to be your *best* friend. Your friendship matters so much to Him. He wants you to come to Him and talk with Him and spend time together. Think about how you can be a good friend to Jesus today.

Thank You for Your friendship, Jesus.
You are my very best friend, and I'm thankful
I get to spend time with You every day.

Feelings Aren't Your Boss

We know that our old life, our old sinful self, was nailed to the cross with Christ. And so the power of sin that held us was destroyed. Sin is no longer our boss.

Romans 6:6

Have you ever been really mad at someone? Maybe at a brother or sister, a friend, or even a parent? Can you remember what happened? Usually when we get really mad it's because we didn't get our own way in a situation. The great news is that because of Jesus, those angry feelings, like sin, don't have to control your life! That's good, because your whole body can feel yucky when you're mad, and angry tears can even give you a headache! In those situations when you're tempted to get mad, remember what Jesus did for you on the cross. Ask Him to help you calm down and to fill your heart with His love instead. Your feelings matter to God.

God, thank You for forgiving me for the times I've let anger take control of me. Fill me with Your love instead.

A Great Reminder

You are now children of God because you have put your trust in Christ Jesus.
GALATIANS 3:26

We've talked a lot about who you are and why you matter to God. Today is a reminder of that truth. Find a piece of paper or a sticky note. Copy Galatians 3:26 on it and decorate it with your favorite colors. Then read the verse again. Post it someplace where you'll see it every day. Did you know the Holy Spirit can help you memorize God's Word? As you write this verse down, ask God to help you remember the truth that you are His beloved child. The Holy Spirit will bring it to your mind miraculously every time you need to hear it.

God, thank You for sending Your Holy Spirit to help me remember Your Word. I'm so thankful for the truth that I am Your child and that You love me. Please bring this verse to my mind whenever I need this great reminder.

God's Perfume

We are a sweet smell of Christ that reaches up to God. It reaches out to those who are being saved from the punishment of sin and to those who are still lost in sin.
2 Corinthians 2:15

Does someone you love wear a special perfume or cologne that makes you happy as soon as they walk into a room? Do you love the smell of fresh cookies baking or your favorite dinner in the oven? Those smells spread throughout the whole house, don't they? Smells can be really good and powerful. The Bible says followers of Jesus have a smell too. This sweet smell reaches all the way up to heaven and out to everyone around. If you have the love of Jesus growing inside you, your sweet smell matters to God and to all the people you know and meet. You are God's perfume. Enjoy spreading this sweetness to others.

God, I'm happy to wear Your perfume!
Let my smell be sweet to everyone around
me and remind them of Your love.

When Troubles Come

If we are children of God, we will receive everything He has promised us. We will share with Christ all the things God has given to Him. But we must share His suffering if we are to share His shining-greatness.

Romans 8:17

Jesus told us we're going to have trouble in this life, so we should expect some days to be hard. But He also said, "Take heart! I have overcome the world" (John 16:33 NIV). How can we live with joy in our hearts while we're expecting trouble? Well, we wake up each morning expecting some challenges, and we ask God to help us through every one of them. That doesn't mean we're grumpy or negative, though. Always look at trouble as a challenge that can be overcome with the power of Christ. Life is an adventure full of both good times and bad. We can find Christ in each moment, and He will give us joy in His presence!

Jesus, I'm expecting some adventures and challenges today, and I know You'll be with me through them all.

Equal in God's Eyes

I praise the Word of God. I praise the Word of the Lord. In God I have put my trust. I will not be afraid. What can man do to me?

Psalm 56:10–11

When you trust God, you don't have to worry about what other people think about you. An old saying goes like this: "We all put our pants on one leg at a time." That means everyone is human. The Bible says God doesn't have favorites (Acts 10:34; Romans 2:11). Or rather, *everyone* is His favorite! You could be a president or a regular person, and it won't matter. That's because everyone is equal in God's eyes. He sees us all just as we are—human. Ask God for help and confidence when you need it around other people. You don't need to be afraid just because someone seems more important than you. You are God's daughter. You are royalty!

Lord, help me be myself around others.
I'm important to You even if others don't see it yet.

The Hands and Feet of Jesus

You are all a part of the body of Christ.
1 Corinthians 12:27

When you choose to follow Jesus, you become part of the body of Christ. In a way, you become the hands and feet of Jesus here on earth until He returns. Saint Teresa of Avila said this: "Christ has no body but yours, no hands, no feet on earth but yours, yours are the eyes with which He looks compassion on this world; yours are the feet with which He walks to do good, yours are the hands, with which He blesses all the world." God wants to use you to carry out His work on earth. That's a pretty big deal! How can you use your hands and feet (and mind and heart) to bring the love of Jesus to others today?

Lord, please show me how to love others the way You do. Help me be Your hands and feet here on earth.

What's Next, Papa?

Instead, the Holy Spirit makes us His sons,
and we can call to Him, "My Father."
ROMANS 8:15

Take a look at the Message paraphrase of Romans 8:15–17:

> *This resurrection life you received from God is not a timid, grave-tending life. It's adventurously expectant, greeting God with a childlike "What's next, Papa?" God's Spirit touches our spirits and confirms who we really are. We know who he is, and we know who we are: Father and children. And we know we are going to get what's coming to us—an unbelievable inheritance! We go through exactly what Christ goes through. If we go through the hard times with him, then we're certainly going to go through the good times with him!*

God wants to have this kind of adventurous relationship with you! A loving Father-daughter relationship where you can go to Him every day about anything.

Lord, thanks for loving me and being
with me on every adventure I take.
I'm so glad You're my heavenly Papa!

Love and Hope

God wants these great riches of the hidden truth to be made known to the people who are not Jews. The secret is this: Christ in you brings hope of all the great things to come.
COLOSSIANS 1:27

The Holy Spirit fills our hearts with the love of God. And that same power is what gives us hope. Romans 15:13 (NLT) says, "I pray that God, the source of hope, will fill you completely with joy and peace because you trust in him. Then you will overflow with confident hope through the power of the Holy Spirit."

When you fill a glass to the very top with water, what happens if you jiggle the glass a little? The water overflows! The Holy Spirit wants to fill you up just like that, so love and hope overflow from you and sprinkle a little on everyone around you.

God, source of hope, please fill me up to the top with love, joy, and peace so I can sprinkle Your love all around me.

A Living Hope

When we have learned not to give up, it shows we have stood the test. When we have stood the test, it gives us hope. Hope never makes us ashamed because the love of God has come into our hearts through the Holy Spirit Who was given to us.

Romans 5:4–5

Jesus gives us a living hope, and because of Him we can have a real-life relationship with God. Our hope of heaven never goes away, but we can also have great hope and peace right now. We don't have to wait for heaven to know God and experience His love, joy, power, and peace. He wants to give that to you now—today! Do you know what faithfulness means? It means God always keeps His promises and that He'll be with you always. Romans 8:28 tells us God is always working everything out for our good, even the tough stuff.

God, thank You for keeping Your promises and being faithful to me always. I'm so glad I get to know You right now.

The Promise

The Holy Spirit was given to us as a promise that we will receive everything God has for us. God's Spirit will be with us until God finishes His work of making us complete. God does this to show His shining-greatness.

Ephesians 1:14

Have you ever made a promise to someone? Did you keep it? Sometimes it's hard for people to even make promises because they don't know what might happen in the future that could change their minds. But God makes promises, and He always keeps them! He put His Spirit in your heart as a promise that He would start working in your heart, and He promises to continue to do that for the rest of your life. Philippians 1:6 tells us God will finish what He started in us. You never have to worry about God giving up on you. He never will!

Thank You, Lord, for my faith. I'm glad I'm Your child and that You've filled me with Your life and hope. I trust that You'll finish the work You've started in me.

All Things Are Possible

Jesus looked at them and said, "This cannot be done by men. But with God all things can be done."
MATTHEW 19:26

Jesus wants to talk to you every single day. Can you hear Him? Sometimes it helps to picture Jesus in your mind. After all, God created your imagination for a reason! He is a personal God. He wants to be your friend and your trusted counselor. He wants you to come to Him first for advice. What do you need advice about today? Ask Jesus for help and guidance. Talk to Him like you would talk to your best friend. You can talk to Him out loud, or you can pray in your heart and mind. It's also helpful to write down your prayers as a reminder of what you prayed. Then you can also write down how God answers your every request, whether His answer is yes, no, or wait.

Jesus, thanks for creating my imagination so I can see and hear from You!

Prayer Is Power

But we have power over all these things through Jesus Who loves us so much.
Romans 8:37

Praying to God is not like sending a quick wish list up to heaven. Nope, God wants your prayer to be a powerful conversation between you and your Creator. You talk, He listens. He talks, you listen. Lots of Christians have trouble with this truth, so it's important to learn how to talk to Jesus now while you're young. Talk to Him now in your mind and heart or out loud, and then wait for His response. He wants to be your loving parent and best friend. Sometimes He will point you to a scripture. Sometimes He will put a picture in your imagination. He might put a worship song in your mind. He may impress your heart with a strong idea or thought. The ways our Creator can speak to us are unlimited.

God, I believe in the power of prayer. I want to hear from You in any way You want to speak to me.

A Life of Purpose

God is the One Who makes our faith and your faith strong in Christ. He has set us apart for Himself.

2 Corinthians 1:21

Jesus saves us and delivers us from our fears so we can live a life of purpose. That's another way of saying that you matter a whole bunch to Jesus and that He has really great plans for your life!

Second Timothy 1:9 (AMP) says, "He delivered us and saved us and called us with a holy calling [a calling that leads to a consecrated life—a life set apart—a life of purpose]." Ask Jesus to make His purpose for you clear. What are your gifts and talents? What brings you joy? Pray and listen as God writes His purpose on your heart. He will continue to let you know about your purpose throughout your life.

Lord, I want to hear from You about my purpose. I'm excited about the plans You have for me! I want to live a life set apart for You.

Like the Wind

Men cannot say they do not know about God. From the beginning of the world, men could see what God is like through the things He has made. This shows His power that lasts forever. It shows that He is God.

Romans 1:20

Sometimes it can be hard to believe in a God we can't see—especially for grown-ups! But the Bible says if we look at all the amazing things God made (including you and all the other humans around you), we are without excuse when it comes to knowing that God is real. Think about the wind. Have you ever actually seen it? Nope, because it's invisible. But when you see the branches of trees swaying, you know the wind is there. That's kind of like God! You can't see Him, but you still know He's there. Think about some friends or family members who don't believe in God. Ask God to open their eyes to see Him in creation.

Thanks for showing Yourself to us in creation, God. Help all my friends and family believe in You too.

The Temple of God

God bought you with a great price.
So honor God with your body. You belong to Him.
1 Corinthians 6:20

When you commit your life to Christ, His Spirit miraculously comes to live inside you, and you become a temple of the Holy Spirit. Isn't that amazing? So if your own body is a place where God dwells, doesn't that make you want to take care of it a little bit better? Your body matters to God. You can take care of your temple by eating right, exercising, getting enough rest, and keeping yourself pure. Being a temple of the Holy Spirit is a big responsibility, and you can't do it without supernatural help.

God, help me take Your words seriously.
I believe I am Your temple, and I want
to make healthy choices for my body.
Please help me remember this every day.

The Race of Life

"Do not fear, for I am with you. Do not be afraid, for I am your God. I will give you strength, and for sure I will help you. Yes, I will hold you up with My right hand that is right and good."

ISAIAH 41:10

When you choose to follow Jesus, you don't have to figure things out on your own. In the book *Discipled by Jesus*, author Robert Gelinas says Jesus doesn't just hand us a baton, like in a relay race, and then leave us to run the rest of the way by ourselves. No, life with Jesus is more like a three-legged race. In that kind of race, one of your legs is tied to another person's leg, and the two of you side hug. Then you have to run in sync with each other. You matter to Jesus, and just like that, He's with you in this race called "life."

Jesus, thank You for being right next to me in everything I do. Thank You that I never have to be afraid.

Live Your Life

Everyone should live the life the Lord gave to him. He should live as he was when he became a Christian. This is what I teach in all the churches.
1 CORINTHIANS 7:17

Only one of you exists—and God made you exactly the way He wanted you to be for a reason. That's why He also wants you to be content with who you are. You look the way you do and were placed where you are for a reason. God wants you to be content with the life He's given you and not wish for someone else's life. He made you unique, and you are absolutely beautiful in His eyes. Your life matters to God, and He has plans and purposes just for you!

Lord, help me embrace the body and the life You gave me, even the parts I have a hard time liking. Help me not to compare what You've given me with what You've given others. I know I'm Your unique creation.

A Child of Light

"You are the light of the world. You cannot hide a city that is on a mountain."
MATTHEW 5:14

Ephesians 5:8 (ESV) says, "For at one time you were darkness, but now you are light in the Lord. Walk as children of light." First Thessalonians 5:5 (ESV) tells us something similar: "For you are all children of light, children of the day." The Bible says you are a child of God, a child of light. Ask the Holy Spirit to remind you of this and help you believe this truth in your heart. Can you picture yourself bringing God's light into dark places? This is one of God's purposes for you. How does that make you feel? Remember, God promises to be with you always!

Light of the world, thank You for planting Your light in my heart. Remind me that I'm Your beloved child, a child of light. Help me walk in Your ways and carry Your light with me wherever I go.

The Helper

"The Helper is the Holy Spirit. The Father will send Him in My place. He will teach you everything and help you remember everything I have told you."
John 14:26

You matter to God so much that He sent you a helper, the Holy Spirit. The Holy Spirit is our counselor, teacher, comforter, and guide. The Holy Spirit is the power of God alive inside everyone who believes in Jesus and chooses to follow Him. How amazing is that? Today we'll take some extra time in prayer to thank God for sending us a helper.

Jesus, thank You for sending me the Holy Spirit as my helper and guide. You've given me every single thing I need to live my life for You. You've thought of everything! When I don't know what to do, I can ask You. When I don't know what to pray, You help. Come, Holy Spirit. Fill my heart with the presence of God. Lead me and guide me as I walk this path with You.

Your Safe Place

God is our safe place and our strength.
He is always our help when we are in trouble.
So we will not be afraid, even if the earth is shaken
and the mountains fall into the center of the sea.
Psalm 46:1–2

What comes to your mind when you think of a safe place? Your house? Your bedroom? A hideout you've made? The Bible says God is our real safe place. As you grow up, your physical safe places will change as you grow, move, and change, but your safe place in God will never change. You can always count on Him, and you never have to be afraid when He's close. He wants to protect you and comfort you, and He wants to tell you how loved you are. Sometimes sitting in the quiet with God is the best way to pray. Ask Him to fill you with His love as you sit in His presence. Picture yourself climbing into His lap and letting Him love you.

Thanks for always being a
safe place for me, God!

Squishy Grapes

"I am the Vine and you are the branches.
Get your life from Me. Then I will live
in you and you will give much fruit.
You can do nothing without Me."
JOHN 15:5

Jesus was the best storyteller. He told stories about everyday things people could understand—like grapes! When you bring grapes home from the store, most of the fresh, juicy fruit is still attached to the vine. But the grapes that have fallen off are usually squishy and gross at the bottom of the bag. That's because they aren't connected to the vine anymore. Jesus says our lives are like those grapes. When we stay connected to Him, we're fresh and full of life. But if we try to live our life apart from Jesus, our life will shrivel up like those squishy grapes at the bottom of the bag. It matters to Jesus that you stay close to Him.

Jesus, show me how to stay close to You and get true life from You. I want to be fresh and full of Your life.

Hearing from God

"My sheep hear My voice and
I know them. They follow Me."
JOHN 10:27

Through Jesus, God created and saved the world. Ask a parent to help you find Hebrews 1:1–3 in the Message paraphrase of the Bible online or on a Bible app. What did you learn from reading it? Here's a summary of what it says: Jesus is God in a human body. When you look at Jesus, you get a clear picture of God, and God can speak directly to you. You may not hear an out-loud voice, but Jesus can speak to your heart just the same. It matters to God that you learn how to hear from Him clearly. Getting to know the voice of God is one of life's greatest adventures.

Jesus, I want to know Your voice. Help me recognize You as You speak to me. Help me pay attention when You're talking to me so I can know Your voice better and better as I grow up. Show me that it's really You.

Created in the Image of God

And God made man in His own likeness. In the likeness of God He made him. He made both male and female.

Genesis 1:27

The book of Genesis tells us we're created in the image of God. Human life is special and honored above every other living thing because each of us bears the mark of our Creator. Just like a valuable piece of artwork, every human being is special because of who made us. We are God's creation. So as you grow up, it's important to remember that every human has value because they are made in the image of God. When you see someone new on the playground, don't look at her shoes and clothes first. Instead, get in the habit of seeing other people as God's precious works of art. Even if they don't see it or believe it, you know it's true. This will begin to change how you treat everyone around you!

Lord, help me treat other people
like they matter, because they do.
We are all Your precious works of art.

God Answers

"Call to Me, and I will answer you. And I will show you great and wonderful things which you do not know."
JEREMIAH 33:3

God promises to answer you when you call on Him! That's an important promise to remember for the rest of your life. As you grow up, on many days you'll be tempted to doubt God's love for you or doubt His voice in your life. That's why it's so important to learn how to hear God now, while you're young. What you hear from Jesus will match what the Bible says. If it doesn't match, watch out. But if you're just not sure if something is from your imagination or if it's from God, simply ask Him. God is real, and He will show you what He wants you to know. God's power is unlimited, and He will always be there for you.

Jesus, I believe You are all-powerful and that You keep Your promises. I believe You want me to hear Your voice and know when You're speaking to me.

Strength Comes from God

I can do all things because
Christ gives me the strength.
Philippians 4:13

Have you been working hard at something lately? Maybe at school or in a sport or with music or art lessons? Are you trying to make yourself stronger in those areas? That's great! The important thing to remember is that strength comes from God. He can help! He wants to be part of everything in your life. When it's time to get ready for lessons or practice, remember that God is with you. Ask Him to help you think clearly and do your best. Talk to Him in your heart and mind during your classes and events. He can help you be a shining light to everyone around you. The hobbies and classes you're good at are not just about you. God wants to use your gifts and talents to spread His love to everyone in your life.

God, thank You for giving me strength in all areas of my life. Let me spread Your love with my gifts and talents.

Jesus Is Close

The eyes of the Lord are on those who do what is right and good. His ears are open to their cry. . . . The Lord is near to those who have a broken heart. And He saves those who are broken in spirit.

Psalm 34:15, 18

Have you ever had a really sad day? That matters to Jesus. Even though you can't physically touch Him, Jesus is even closer than you think. When your heart is broken, Jesus is with you. When your spirit feels crushed, God is close. God's Word says He hears your prayers and that His eyes are on you. He hears you and sees you. You're important to Him, and He loves you more than you could ever imagine. Sometimes God will send someone to give you a hug and an extraspecial dose of love at just the right time. And sometimes He'll supernaturally warm your heart with love as you talk to Him.

Jesus, thanks for loving me and caring for me when I'm sad. Help me know that You are near.

Power and Love

But the Lord is the true God. He is the living God and the King Who lives forever. . . . It is He Who made the earth by His power, and the world by His wisdom. By His understanding He has spread out the heavens. When He speaks, there is a storm of waters in the heavens. He makes the clouds rise from the ends of the earth. He makes lightning for the rain, and brings out the wind from His store-houses.

Jeremiah 10:10, 12–13

The God who loves you and cares about you is the same God who stretched out the heavens. How amazing is that? It might be hard to believe that you matter so much to God, but the Bible says it's true. When you think about God's unlimited power and His love for you, do you trust that God can handle anything you've got going on?

God, if You can speak water into existence at the sound of Your voice, I know You can take care of anything that comes my way.

God Sings

"The Lord your God is with you, a Powerful One Who wins the battle. He will have much joy over you. With His love He will give you new life. He will have joy over you with loud singing."
ZEPHANIAH 3:17

Getting to know God through reading His Word and praying will change your life. That's because when you do those things, He changes your thoughts to match His thoughts. As you get to know God, you'll find He's so much more than you ever thought possible. He is all-knowing, all-powerful, and the Savior of the world, and yet the Bible says He sings over us! God delights in you. He is proud of you. He sees you through the eyes of Jesus. Nothing can make Him love you more or less. You cannot work for God's love. It just is.

Lord, I want to know Your words and Your truth for my life. I accept Your great love for me. I praise You and thank You for caring about me and showing me Your ways.

A Place to Hide

You are my hiding place. You keep me safe from trouble. All around me are your songs of being made free. I will show you and teach you in the way you should go. I will tell you what to do with My eye upon you.

PSALM 32:7–8

Have you ever played the game sardines? One person hides and everyone else has to find the hider and hide with them until only one person is left looking. It's a lot more fun to play sardines than to play regular hide-and-seek. Why? Because you aren't hiding alone. You get to hide with someone else. The Bible says God is our hiding place. He always wants to be found. It sure is nice to never have to hide alone—especially in the dark! God is always with you, so you're never alone. God will protect you and show you which way to go next.

Thank You for being a safe place
for me to hide, Lord. I'm so thankful
that I never have to hide alone.

The Return Line

He answered me, "I am all you need. I give you My loving-favor. My power works best in weak people." I am happy to be weak and have troubles so I can have Christ's power in me. . . . For when I am weak, then I am strong.

2 Corinthians 12:9–10

Have you ever gone back to a store with a grown-up to return something that didn't fit right? Those return lines at the store can get pretty long, especially right after Christmas! God likes to exchange things too: old for new, death for life, ashes for beauty, sadness for joy, despair for praise (see Isaiah 61:3). He also exchanges our weakness for His strength. Can you picture yourself taking everything you're not so good at and laying it at Jesus' feet? What does He want to give you instead? Ask Him!

God, I'm so thankful that You can turn my darkness into light, my sadness into joy, my ashes into beauty, and my weakness into Your strength. Please show me what You'd like to exchange in my life.

Anytime

Let us go with complete trust to the throne of God. We will receive His loving-kindness and have His loving-favor to help us whenever we need it.

Hebrews 4:16

You've probably seen some movies about a princess, right? Which one is your favorite? Have you seen one where the common people need special permission to go into the palace to see the king or queen? And when they do, they bow low before the throne and talk in special ways to show respect. Of course, God will always deserve our respect, but we don't need special permission to go into His presence! The Message paraphrase of Hebrews 4:16 says, "So let's walk right up to him and get what he is so ready to give. Take the mercy, accept the help." Because of Jesus, you can walk right up to God and talk to Him—anytime of day, anywhere. You don't have to dress up or anything! God is always available to talk with you.

God, I'm so glad I can talk to You anytime I want to and need to.

His Girl

"Do not be afraid. For I have bought you and made you free. I have called you by name. You are Mine! . . . You are of great worth in My eyes. You are honored and I love you."
ISAIAH 43:1, 4

Can you picture Jesus saying these words to you? How do they make you feel? Do you believe God loves you this much? When you believe you're who God says you are, everything in your life changes! Let Him speak to your heart every day to remind you of your worth and how much you matter to Him. Before you get out of bed every morning, thank God for a new day and ask Him to remind you of the truth: you are His girl, His beloved daughter. That's why you have nothing to be afraid of. And God is always with you. Ask Him to help you believe these truths and to live your life like you believe them.

I am Yours, Lord God. Please remind me of this truth every morning.

Lots of Choices

Trust in the Lord with all your heart, and do not trust in your own understanding. Agree with Him in all your ways, and He will make your paths straight.

Proverbs 3:5–6

As you grow up, you'll have lots of choices to make. But God will help you with them all. Isaiah 30:21 (NIV) says, "Whether you turn to the right or to the left, your ears will hear a voice behind you, saying, 'This is the way; walk in it.'" When we forget that God wants to help us make good choices, we can get confused and worried. When we leave God out of the decision-making process, it can cause lots of unnecessary problems. Are you planning a birthday party? Ask God to be a part of it. Who does He want you to invite? What other choices do you need to make soon? Invite Jesus in.

Jesus, I ask You to be a part of every single thing I have going on. I trust You to help me make good choices.

No Worries

In truthful speech and in the power of God; with weapons of righteousness in the right hand and in the left. . . sorrowful, yet always rejoicing; poor, yet making many rich; having nothing, and yet possessing everything.

2 Corinthians 6:7, 10 niv

Do you worry about what others are saying and thinking about you? Second Corinthians 6:8 (nlt) says, "We serve God whether people honor us or despise us, whether they slander us or praise us." When God's power is at work in you, you can be confident in who you are as His child no matter what anyone else thinks. When other kids say bad things about you, it can definitely hurt. But as you take those hurts to Jesus, He reminds you of the truth. You are a dearly loved daughter of the King of kings! You have access to all of God's power. You can walk right up to Him because of how loved you are.

Lord, thank You that I never have to worry about what other people think of me. That's because I'm Your beloved child.

Keep Your Chin Up and Sing!

The Lord is my strength and my safe cover. My heart trusts in Him, and I am helped. So my heart is full of joy. I will thank Him with my song.

Psalm 28:7

Being confident in who you are in Christ comes from spending time with God in worship, in His Word, and in prayer. This God-confidence allows you to keep your chin up when things around you seem out of control or way too big and overwhelming. And it almost always helps to sing when life feels a little wobbly! Turn on some praise music and sing your heart out to God. When we worship God, He fills us with peace and joy no matter what's going on around us. Nehemiah 8:10 (niv) says, "Do not grieve, for the joy of the Lord is your strength."

Lord, thank You that Your joy gives me strength and confidence no matter what is happening around me. I will give thanks to You while I sing.

No One Like Him

There is no one like You among the gods,
O Lord. And there are no works like Yours.
All the nations You have made will come and
worship before You, O Lord. And they will
bring honor to Your name. For You are great
and do great things. You alone are God.
Psalm 86:8–10

The time you spend with God will accomplish more than anything else you could ever do, because no one can do what He can do. Jeremiah 32:17 (ESV) says, "Ah, Lord God! It is you who have made the heavens and the earth by your great power and by your outstretched arm! Nothing is too hard for you." Ask God to help you believe that He can do anything! No problem is too hard, too big, or too small for God to help.

God of all creation, no one is like You.
I am so blessed to be able to take
everything on my heart to You in prayer
and to know that You want to help me!

Ask and Receive

"I say to you, ask, and what you ask for will be given to you. Look, and what you are looking for you will find. Knock, and the door you are knocking on will be opened to you. For everyone who asks, will receive what he asks for. Everyone who looks, will find what he is looking for. Everyone who knocks, will have the door opened to him."

Luke 11:9–10

Let's take a deep look into this important scripture passage for the next few days. Does this scripture mean God is going to give us everything we want? No, it means He wants the very best for us and always wants to help us. James 4:2 (NIV) says, "You do not have because you do not ask God." Too often we forget to go to God first. We try to get our needs met by other people or from things when God is just waiting for us to come to Him.

Lord, please help me go to You first with all my wants and needs. I know You want to help me.

Look and Find

"You will look for Me and find Me,
when you look for Me with all your heart."
Jeremiah 29:13

What do seeking God and looking for Him with all your heart mean? Check out the following verses that help us understand. The Lord is speaking in the first two.

- "I love those who love me, and those who seek me diligently find me." Proverbs 8:17 ESV
- "But seek first the kingdom of God and his righteousness, and all these things will be added to you." Matthew 6:33 ESV
- "Seek the Lord and his strength; seek his presence continually!" 1 Chronicles 16:11 ESV
- "Come near to God and he will come near to you." James 4:8 NIV

Seeking and looking for God are all about loving God and staying close to Him. As you look for God, you'll find that He's everywhere. God is close—not far away—and He wants to be found!

Thank You for being close to me, Lord.
Help me look for You in everything.

Knock, Knock

"See! I stand at the door and knock.
If anyone hears My voice and opens the door,
I will come in to him and we will eat together."
REVELATION 3:20

Who's there? Jesus! The Bible tells us we can knock on God's door and be invited in, but did you know Jesus is knocking on your door too? Today's scripture tells us this truth. Whenever you play hide-and-seek, wouldn't the game be so much easier if the person who's supposed to be hiding is looking for you too? That's the really amazing thing: while we're looking for God, He's looking for us. He wants you to find Him, and He makes it pretty simple. If you look for Him, you'll find Him. Jesus is always knocking at the door of your heart. Do you hear Him? Will you let Him in?

Jesus, thanks for looking for me. I'm so glad You want me to find You! You've knocked on my heart, and I'm letting You in.

Gardening with God

Do not be fooled. You cannot fool God.
A man will get back whatever he plants!
GALATIANS 6:7

Do you like to grow things? You've probably learned about planting seeds in school, and maybe you've even watched a plant grow week by week. Jesus liked to use gardening illustrations to help people understand what He was teaching. Have you ever heard of the gardening words *sowing* and *reaping*? The law of sowing and reaping means what you plant is what you harvest. It's true in the natural world, and it's true in the spiritual world. If you plant pumpkins, you'll harvest pumpkins. And if you plant doubt and worry in your heart, that's exactly what will grow. Your heart matters so much to God, and He wants to plant really good things there. Let's garden with God this week. Are you ready?

Jesus, I ask You to prepare the soil of my heart for the good things You want to plant there. Pluck out the weeds and help me sow good plants instead.

Fresh Fruit

But the fruit that comes from having the Holy Spirit in our lives is: love, joy, peace, not giving up, being kind, being good, having faith, being gentle, and being the boss over our own desires.
GALATIANS 5:22–23

Do you have a favorite fruit? It tastes the best when it's ripe and fresh, right? The Bible talks about a different kind of fruit—spiritual fruit. When we invite Jesus into our hearts, His presence within us starts changing and transforming us, and this produces fresh, spiritual fruit as we become more like Him. We matter so much to God that He wants to plant these special fruits in our hearts. In Matthew 7:20, Jesus says we can recognize people by their fruit. People who make good choices produce good fruit. People who make bad choices produce yucky fruit. Ask God to show you if you're producing good spiritual fruit. Let's talk about these special fruits for the next few days.

God, I want to produce fresh, healthy fruit so others can see You are at work in me.

The Love Fruit

Those who do not love do not know
God because God is love.
1 John 4:8

The first fruit of the Spirit is love. Did you know that the biblical definition of love is God? God = love. Love = God. Most people think love is a feeling of happiness, but that's not always true. Love is a choice. You can still choose to love someone even if you don't feel like it. First Corinthians 13:4–8 (NIV) tells us more about what true love is like: "Love is patient, love is kind. It does not envy, it does not boast, it is not proud. It does not dishonor others, it is not self-seeking, it is not easily angered, it keeps no record of wrongs. Love does not delight in evil but rejoices with the truth. It always protects, always trusts, always hopes, always perseveres. Love never fails." This is the kind of love fruit Jesus will start creating in you as you follow Him.

God, please grow more love in
my heart as I follow You.

The Joy Fruit

For the holy nation of God is not food and drink. It is being right with God. It is peace and joy given by the Holy Spirit.
ROMANS 14:17

You have a choice every day when you wake up. You can choose to be thankful for a new day and look at it with joy and hopefulness, or you can choose to be grumpy. The second choice happens a lot if you aren't careful and allow yourself to be full of stress and worry instead of looking at each moment as a gift. Ask God to fill you with the fruit of joy and to help you see each new day as a gift. When you wake up, ask Him to go before you and remind you that God's Spirit is always with you. Then as you look for Him, you'll be able to see the little blessings God sends your way.

God, please fill me with the fruit of joy
so my attitude is a reflection of You.

The Peace Fruit

The peace of God is much greater than the human mind can understand. This peace will keep your hearts and minds through Christ Jesus.
PHILIPPIANS 4:7

The fruit of peace is a supernatural ability to stay calm in the middle of anything, and God's peace in the middle of problems is beyond what any human can understand. God has to grow this special fruit in your heart. He asks us to replace all our worries with His peace through prayer. So instead of complaining or being afraid when you're feeling crummy about something, talk to God. Tell Him what's on your mind and thank Him for what He's done and what He will do. That's when God will supernaturally change your worries into peace. And this is a true and lasting peace, not just a feel-good moment.

God, please grow Your peace in my heart. Help me replace worry with thankfulness. I trust You to give me true, lasting peace when I ask You to do that. Thank You for loving me so much!

The Patience Fruit

God has chosen you. You are holy and loved by Him. . . .
You should be kind to others and have no pride.
Be gentle and be willing to wait for others.
COLOSSIANS 3:12

Patience can be a difficult fruit to grow! But it's a spiritual fruit God wants us to have. Check out these verses about patience:

- "We continue to shout our praise even when we're hemmed in with troubles, because we know how troubles can develop passionate patience in us." Romans 5:3 MSG
- "Be completely humble and gentle; be patient, bearing with one another in love." Ephesians 4:2 NIV
- "Be patient with each person, attentive to individual needs. And be careful that when you get on each other's nerves you don't snap at each other. Look for the best in each other, and always do your best to bring it out." 1 Thessalonians 5:14–15 MSG

If you're having trouble growing the fruit of patience, ask God for help!

Lord, I admit I struggle with waiting. I need Your help growing the fruit of patience in me.

The Kindness Fruit

The Lord came to us from far away, saying, "I have loved you with a love that lasts forever. So I have helped you come to Me with loving-kindness."

JEREMIAH 31:3

God is kind, and His ways are kind. All through the Bible, you'll find examples of God's loving-kindness. God showers love and kindness on us, and the fruit of kindness is important. Why? Because a lot of people in this world still don't know much about God or have the wrong idea about Him. It's our job as His followers to show them who God really is, and one way we can do that is by letting them see our joy. That's one reason He wants the full life John 10:10 mentions for us and for us to live joy-filled lives. If we live with kindness and love in our hearts—and with joy—the people around us will get a true view of God.

Thank You for Your loving-kindness to me, Lord. Please grow this fruit in my heart to share with others.

The Goodness Fruit

Trust in the Lord, and do good.
PSALM 37:3

It's hard to make good choices all the time, right? We definitely need God's help to grow this fruit. First John 5:18 says, "We know that no child of God keeps on sinning. The Son of God watches over him and the devil cannot get near him." We can stay away from sin and make good choices because Jesus protects us from the enemy and helps us turn away from him. The Spirit of God grows the fruit of goodness inside us when we turn to God for help with our choices. We all make mistakes sometimes. When this happens, God wants us to run to Him for help instead of running away. He isn't mad at you. He wants to show you His love and help you make better choices next time.

Lord, thanks for Your forgiveness when I mess up. I'm so thankful You love me and want to help me make better choices. Please grow goodness in my heart.

The Faithfulness Fruit

"His owner said to him, 'You have done well. You are a good and faithful servant. You have been faithful over a few things. I will put many things in your care. Come and share my joy.'"

Matthew 25:21

Faithfulness is another fruit the Holy Spirit will grow in us as we get closer to Jesus. God has given all of us gifts and talents to use to faithfully serve Him and share His love with others. Being faithful means we show up and do what we say we're going to do. We want God to tell us we've done a good job doing His work here. Finishing any job requires lots and lots of faithfulness. And finishing the job well requires lots of prayer and dependence on God. If God gives you something small to do and you do it well, He will trust you to do even greater things.

God, I want to be faithful to You in all things—big and small. Please grow the fruit of faithfulness in me.

The Fruit of Gentleness

Let all people see how gentle you are.
The Lord is coming again soon.
PHILIPPIANS 4:5

The Bible talks quite a bit about being gentle. It's a great fruit that God wants to grow in you. But when our lives get extra busy, we often forget about being gentle. Sometimes we say whatever we feel whether or not it hurts somebody's feelings. But God doesn't want us to live this way. He wants us to be gentle with each other. Just like parents are gentle with their newborn baby, we need to be gentle with our words and actions toward others. If you have something important to say, say it! But say it with gentleness and love in your heart instead of blurting the first thing you think. Take your thoughts to God first and ask Him to help you say them gently.

God, please grow gentleness in my heart.
I want to be kind and gentle with my words
and actions toward everyone around me.

The Fruit of Self-Control

Do your best to add holy living to your faith.
Then add to this a better understanding.
As you have a better understanding, be able to
say no when you need to. Do not give up. And as
you wait and do not give up, live God-like.
2 Peter 1:5–6

In the New International Version of the Bible, 2 Peter 1:5–7 says, "For this very reason, make every effort to add to your faith goodness; and to goodness, knowledge; and to knowledge, self-control; and to self-control, perseverance; and to perseverance, godliness; and to godliness, mutual affection; and to mutual affection, love." That's quite a list! But as the fruits of God's Spirit grow inside you, these values come along too. Sometimes it's hard to have self-control, especially if someone just made fresh cookies! But paying attention to your body is important to help you stay safe and healthy in lots of situations.

Lord, I want to learn how to pay more
attention to what my body is telling me.
Please grow the fruit of self-control in me.

Filled with Fruit

And this is my prayer: I pray that your love will grow more and more. I pray that you will have better understanding and be wise in all things. . . . And I pray that you will be filled with the fruits of right living. These come from Jesus Christ, with honor and thanks to God.

Philippians 1:9, 11

As you've seen over the past week, the fruit of the Spirit is a really big deal! When the Spirit of God is at work in you, special fruits grow. Now that you know more about God's fruit, can you see any fruit already growing in your life? Are the fruits of love, joy, peace, patience, kindness, goodness, faithfulness, gentleness, and self-control taking root and getting bigger in your heart? If so, this brings much glory to God! If you're not sure, though, start talking to God about this. Ask Him to clear out your heart to make room for what He wants to plant there.

God, please fill me up with the fruit of Your Spirit. I want to see You at work in my life.

Gifts and Surprises

God asked me to preach this Good News. He gave me the gift of His loving-favor. He gave me His power to preach it.
EPHESIANS 3:7

The Message translation of Ephesians 3:7 says, "This is my life work: helping people understand and respond to this Message. It came as a sheer gift to me, a real surprise, God handling all the details." When we say yes to God, He blesses us with divine gifts and surprises! Paul, the guy who wrote the book of Ephesians, said his life's work was to help people understand and respond to the gospel of Jesus Christ. Paul didn't feel like he was good enough for this, and God calling him to do this was a real surprise and a gift to him. What gifts has God given you? How do you think He might want to use those gifts to share His love with others now and in the future?

Lord, thank You for the gifts You've given me. I want to use them to show others how much You love them.

Prayer Life

In the morning before the sun was up, Jesus went to a place where He could be alone. He prayed there.

Mark 1:35

The Bible says Jesus often went away to be alone with God and pray. Hopefully, you're beginning to understand how much you matter to God and why it's important to spend time with Him. As a follower of Jesus, your power and hope and strength to make it through each day come from your time spent with God. Jesus lived a life of prayer. How can you live a life of prayer too? By inviting Him into every moment of your day. By seeking His thoughts when you need help. By asking Him to give you love for others as you encounter people during the day. By telling Him you love Him. And by thanking Him for His presence in your life. Try those things right now as you invite Jesus to be a part of your day.

Jesus, I invite You into every moment of my day. Remind me that You are with me at all times.

Worship Matters

Praise the Lord! For it is good to sing praises to our God. For it is pleasing and praise is right. . . . He heals those who have a broken heart. He heals their sorrows. . . . Great is our Lord, and great in power. His understanding has no end.

Psalm 147:1, 3, 5

Do you know what worship means? Maybe you've heard people at church say that when we worship God, we show Him how much He means to us. We show how much we love and adore Him. We do this by living a life of prayer, and we do this by singing to Him and telling Him we love Him. What other ways can you think of to worship God? Worship matters to God. His heart wants to know that we're choosing to love Him above everything else. In your times of prayer, have you ever just praised God instead of asking for things? Try it right now.

God, I love You so much! You are amazing! You've given me life, and I'm so thankful that I can know You personally.

Blessings

Jabez called on the God of Israel, saying, "O, if only You would bring good to me and give me more land! If only Your hand might be with me, that You would keep me from being hurt!" And God gave him what he asked for.

1 Chronicles 4:10

Jabez asked God for a big blessing, and God gave it to him! We see people asking for God's blessing throughout the entire Bible. Does this mean God will always give us everything we ask for? No, because God always sees the big picture. Something we think might be good for us could actually turn out pretty bad. That's why we trust God to say yes or no to everything we ask for. Read Matthew 5 if you want to know more about the blessings of God. Asking for His blessing is asking for His purpose and power in your life, not asking Him to give you everything you want. God knows best.

Lord, I trust You to bless me the way You know is best for my life.

Here for a Purpose

"The God Who made the world and everything in it is the Lord of heaven and earth. He does not live in buildings made by hands."
ACTS 17:24

Check out more of this passage in the New International Version of the Bible: "From one man he made all the nations, that they should inhabit the whole earth; and he marked out their appointed times in history and the boundaries of their lands. God did this so that they would seek him and perhaps reach out for him and find him, though he is not far from any one of us" (verses 26–27). Wow! God knows your name and everything about you. He set you on earth at this exact time in history for a purpose. He wants you to know Him. He wants you to love Him and love others through Him. Does that tell you how much you matter to God, or what?

Lord, sometimes it's still hard for me to believe that You know everything about me and love me anyway. But Your Word tells me it's true. Thank You, God!

Creation Sings

I will sing of the loving-kindness of the Lord forever. I will make known with my mouth how faithful You are to all people. . . . The heavens are Yours; and the earth is Yours. You have made the world and all that is in it.

Psalm 89:1, 11

God shows us how much we matter to Him in so many ways. One of the simplest ways to see His love is to go outside and experience His creation for yourself. You can see God's handiwork in the flowers and trees in spring and summer. In the leaves changing to bright colors in the fall and the blankets of snow He sends in the winter. Animals and creatures great and small know their Creator. The birds God created are always singing His praises as they go about their busy tasks, and you can too. God gave you your voice to talk to Him, to tell of His great love, and to sing His praise.

Thanks for showing Your love for me through Your creation, God. I love to sing Your praise.

The Good Shepherd

"I am the Good Shepherd. The Good Shepherd gives His life for the sheep."
John 10:11

Jesus talked about gardening and farming and herding sheep because He was talking to everyday people. Common people mattered to Jesus, and He wanted them to know His love and His truth. Jesus tells us He is our shepherd. In Jesus' day, a good shepherd loved and cared for his sheep with compassion and kindness. He needed the sheep to listen to him so they could travel to the best places for food. When the shepherd walked ahead of them, they followed him because they knew his voice. Jesus calls us His sheep, and He lovingly cares for us. Today's verse reminds us that our shepherd even gave His very life for us! When we get to know His voice, we can be sure we're following a leader we can trust.

Jesus, You are my loving shepherd. I follow You because I trust You and I know I can count on You to lead me to the right place.

We Are His Sheep

As He saw many people, He had loving-pity on them. They were troubled and were walking around everywhere. They were like sheep without a shepherd.
MATTHEW 9:36

Sheep are born with an instinct to follow. If a sheep does something dangerous or stupid, the sheep behind it usually follow. Sheep need a good leader to follow. When Jesus came to earth, He saw that the people were acting like sheep without a shepherd—making bad choices and following others who were also making bad choices. Some people look at those making bad decisions and judge them harshly, leaving them to their consequences. But not Jesus. The Bible says He had compassion on these people. He knew what caused them to make those choices, and He loved them and wanted to help. We are His sheep, and we matter to Jesus. He came to be the good shepherd, to lead people to Himself.

Jesus, thank You for leading me. Help me be the kind of leader who has compassion and love for others.

Close to the Shepherd

"A man has one hundred sheep and one of them is lost. Will he not leave the ninety-nine and go to the mountains to look for that one lost sheep? If he finds it, for sure, I tell you, he will have more joy over that one, than over the ninety-nine that were not lost. I tell you, My Father in heaven does not want one of these little children to be lost."

MATTHEW 18:12–14

Jesus doesn't want anyone to be left behind. Each child of His matters and is precious and important to Him. Good shepherds don't want to lose any of their sheep. If even one of them wanders off, they'll go searching for it. When we wander off, we can get lost, hurt, and confused. But you matter so much to Jesus that if you ever go wandering off, He'll search for you too! When we stay close to our shepherd in the first place, though, He leads us to the right places.

Jesus, help me stay close to You.
Lead me on the right path.

Close to His Heart

He will feed His flock like a shepherd. He will gather the lambs in His arms and carry them close to His heart. He will be gentle in leading those that are with young.

Isaiah 40:11

When Jesus talks about His sheep, He's talking about you. And He is our gentle shepherd. The Bible says He carries us close to His heart. Let's look at one more verse about shepherding:

> *The Lord is my Shepherd [to feed, to guide and to shield me], I shall not want. He lets me lie down in green pastures; He leads me beside the still and quiet waters. He refreshes and restores my soul (life).*
>
> Psalm 23:1–3 AMP

Can you picture Jesus carrying you close to His heart? Tell Jesus how this makes you feel.

Jesus, You are my gentle shepherd. You are my wise and kind leader. I know You care for me and that You want me to know Your voice. Help me follow close to You.

Be You

Let your light shine in front of men.
Then they will see the good things you do and
will honor your Father Who is in heaven.
MATTHEW 5:16

Do you want to know the best way to share the love of Jesus with others? Be *you*! Simply be the amazing person God created you to be. God gave each of us special gifts to use to glorify Him and show others how amazing He is. Not sure what gifts you have? Ask Jesus to show you the special gifts and talents He put inside you. Ask a parent or another trusted grown-up what makes you special. A lot of times, other people can see what's so special about us better than we can. Jesus wants you to know what makes you special! So go find out, and then use those special gifts to spread His love.

Jesus, please open my eyes and heart to see the ways You made me special. Help me be brave as I use these special gifts to be like You.

More Than Anything

Your eyes saw me before I was put together.
And all the days of my life were written in
Your book before any of them came to be.
PSALM 139:16

Have you ever felt like you don't really matter? Check out what David in the Bible said to God, which is also true about you: "For you created my inmost being; you knit me together in my mother's womb. I praise you because I am fearfully and wonderfully made; your works are wonderful, I know that full well" (Psalm 139:13–14 NIV). Imagine Jesus putting you together as you were growing in your mom's body. He knows everything about you, and He cares for you and all His children more than anything else in creation. You are so important to Him that He died for you on the cross so you could be with Him forever. The next time you're feeling down or unimportant, remember who made you and how much He loves you!

Jesus, it makes me feel so good
that I matter to You. Thanks!

The Power of Prayer

And pray for each other so you may be healed. The prayer from the heart of a man right with God has much power.
James 5:16

The Bible tells us prayer is powerful! The Amplified Bible explains James 5:16 a bit more: "The heartfelt and persistent prayer of a righteous man (believer) can accomplish much [when put into action and made effective by God—it is dynamic and can have tremendous power]." Your prayers matter to God, and they can accomplish a lot! Not only do we get to know God better when we talk to Him, but our prayers can make things happen. God's Word tells us to pray for others so they can be healed. This means physical bodies can be healed but also that broken hearts can be mended. Do you know anyone who has an illness or disease? Anyone who is sad or lonely? Pray for them! They matter to Jesus.

Thank You that my prayers matter to You, God! I pray for my friends and family who need Your powerful healing in their lives.

How You Treat Others Matters to God

"You will be guilty of the same things you find in others. When you say what is wrong in others, your words will be used to say what is wrong in you."
Matthew 7:2

It's not easy to put yourself in someone else's shoes. And the Bible warns against judging others. Judging means you form a strong opinion about someone, and when you judge them without understanding their situation, you don't show the love of Jesus. The mean girl at school? She might not have a mom who loves her, and she only knows how to express herself through anger. The boy who smells bad and wears dirty clothes? His dad may have lost his job and his family can't afford deodorant—or maybe their water was shut off! You just never know. So pray for others who seem to be struggling and ask God how you can love them better.

Dear God, please help me not to judge others. I want to be a loving example of You to everyone I see each day.

Your Tears Matter

You have seen how many places I have gone. Put my tears in Your bottle. Are they not in Your book? Then those who hate me will turn back when I call. I know that God is for me.

Psalm 56:8–9

Does God care about what makes you sad? Yes. The Bible says He counts your tears and writes them down. Man of Sorrows was one of Jesus' nicknames. That was because He was rejected by people (even by some of His own friends) and He was familiar with pain and sadness. Whatever you're going through, Jesus understands because He's been there. Have you ever felt left out or not good enough for other people? Talk to God about it. Your tears matter to Him. Revelation 21:4 gives us hope for the future in heaven: "God will take away all their tears. There will be no more death or sorrow or crying or pain."

Lord, thank You for Your promises. I'm so glad You're with me and that You care about what makes me sad. Please help my heart feel better.

Take a Breath

"Come to Me, all of you who work and have heavy loads. I will give you rest."
MATTHEW 11:28

Sometimes you get tired. Kids have lots of responsibilities at school and home. Then add extra stuff like soccer or ballet or karate, and life can get really busy! Take a look at what else Jesus says in Matthew 11: "I'll show you how to take a real rest. Walk with me and work with me—watch how I do it. Learn the unforced rhythms of grace. I won't lay anything heavy or ill-fitting on you. Keep company with me and you'll learn to live freely and lightly" (verses 29–30 MSG). Your busyness matters to Jesus. He wants you to come to Him and rest in Him daily. Does that mean you have to take a nap? Nope. It means Jesus wants you to relax and know that He's with you, always taking care of you.

Jesus, please help me relax and take a deep breath. You've got this. And You've always got me.

Joy and Blessing

Those who have a pure heart are happy,
because they will see God.
MATTHEW 5:8

The Bible talks a lot about being "blessed" and having joy. When Jesus talks about having joy, He's talking about a deep understanding that Jesus is with us and making everything right—no matter what. That means even if you're having a really bad day, you can still have joy. Why? Because of this promise from God: "And we know that in all things God works for the good of those who love him, who have been called according to his purpose" (Romans 8:28 NIV). You matter to God, and He's working everything out for your good, even when things don't seem to be going your way. So trust Him to do that. He will!

Jesus, I want to get closer to You every day. Please fill me with Your kind of joy no matter what kind of day I'm having. Help me trust that You're working everything out for my good.

Saying Hello

"If you say hello only to the people you like,
are you doing any more than others?
The people who do not know God do that much."
MATTHEW 5:47

Have you ever felt left out? It doesn't feel good, does it? Jesus wants us to show other people that they matter to Him too. He wants us to include others and be kind to them, even if they don't happen to be our best friends. Maybe nobody likes a girl in your class, and she's always sitting alone. Can Jesus give you the courage to go say hello with a smile? Yes, of course He can. You might even make a new friend and discover that you have a lot in common. Sometimes people sit alone because they're shy and afraid. Can you pray for that person to feel loved and accepted?

Jesus, please fill me with Your power and courage to love others, even when I don't feel like it or when it might be embarrassing. Help me see others as You see them.

No Worries

"Do not worry about tomorrow. Tomorrow will have its own worries. The troubles we have in a day are enough for one day."
MATTHEW 6:34

Have you ever been really worried about something? Maybe about a test at school or going to the doctor to get a shot? It's really easy to make yourself nervous about something. But Jesus cares about you so much that He tells you not to worry. Why? Because worrying is bad for your body. Worrying can cause your body to release stress hormones that make your heart work harder, cause you to be tired and grumpy, and even slow down your body's ability to fight illness and disease. So Jesus simply tells us not to do it! He wants you to have His peace even in scary situations.

Jesus, I know You are strong enough to handle all my worries. I bring each of them to You, and I ask You to replace those worries with the peace that comes from trusting You.

The Golden Rule Matters

"Do for other people whatever you would like to have them do for you."
MATTHEW 7:12

Have you heard of the Golden Rule? This rule has been around since ancient times, and most people, whether or not they go to church, know what it means. The Golden Rule means treating others as you would want them to treat you. This applies to friends, family members—everyone! Treating others well matters to God. The next time you're having a great time with friends or family and someone suddenly gets upset, stop and think about the Golden Rule. Is everyone treating each other the way they like to be treated? If not, let them know about the Golden Rule and ask Jesus for help putting it into practice.

Jesus, I want to follow the Golden Rule. I want to treat others with kindness and respect, the way I like to be treated and the way You treat me! Please help me do that when I'm with my friends and family.

Kids Matter to Jesus

Jesus took a little child and put him among them. He said, "For sure, I tell you, unless you have a change of heart and become like a little child, you will not get into the holy nation of heaven. Whoever is without pride as this little child is the greatest in the holy nation of heaven. Whoever receives a little child because of Me receives Me."

MATTHEW 18:2–5

Jesus loves kids! All through the Bible we see Him caring for children and loving them. In Matthew 19, though, some people tried to stop kids from being with Jesus. This upset Him, and He told them to let the kids come to Him. One reason children are so important to Jesus is that they have a lot to teach the world. That's right! The way you think and believe is the way Jesus wants grown-ups to think and believe. He wants us all to have simple, childlike faith.

Jesus, I'm so thankful that You think I'm important. Thanks again for loving me so well!

The Whole Truth Matters

"Go in through the narrow door. The door is wide and the road is easy that leads to hell. Many people are going through that door. But the door is narrow and the road is hard that leads to life that lasts forever. Few people are finding it."
MATTHEW 7:13–14

As you grow up, you may hear the words "All roads lead to heaven." But Jesus tells us that's not true. Jesus is the only door to heaven, and it matters a lot to Him that you know this truth. Many people don't know the real Jesus and how amazing a friendship with Him can be. Our job as His followers is to love Jesus, love others, and be exactly who God created us to be. When people see that we have a real, everyday friendship with Jesus, they'll want to know about it!

Jesus, help me be the person who shines a bright light toward the narrow door! I want to show Your love to others so they can get to know the real You.

What Really Matters

"Gather together riches in heaven where they will not be eaten by bugs or become rusted. Men cannot break in and steal them. For wherever your riches are, your heart will be there also."

MATTHEW 6:20–21

Have you ever pretended to hunt for buried treasure—for jewels or gold? Jesus tells us about a different kind of treasure. He talks about gathering riches that can never, ever be taken from us. Can you think of what He might mean? Is your family a treasure? Is your friendship with Jesus a treasure? Are you a treasure? Of course! If we become obsessed with things, wanting more and more, our hearts will never be content or happy. But when we treasure Jesus and the people He's put in our life, we will be blessed beyond measure!

Jesus, please help me not obsess with getting more and more things. Things don't really matter. Love matters and people matter. Help me be thankful and content with the blessings You've given me.

Dual Citizenship

But we are citizens of heaven. Christ, the One Who saves from the punishment of sin, will be coming down from heaven again. We are waiting for Him to return.

PHILIPPIANS 3:20

Have you learned about citizenship in school? American citizens have certain rights, freedoms, and responsibilities. Every country has its own laws and rights for its citizens. The Bible tells us that as children of God, we are citizens of heaven. Ephesians 2:6 says even though we live here on earth, we're spiritually sitting with Christ in heaven. That means we're members of both places. So while you're here on earth, you have all the privileges and responsibilities of a princess—a child of the King—at the same time. As you go through your day, remember who you really are. Your earthly citizenship will last for your lifetime, but your heavenly citizenship lasts for eternity.

Lord, thank You for making me Your princess. Show me what it means to live for You while I'm here on earth.

Loving God

"I have loved you just as My Father has loved Me. Stay in My love."
John 15:9

We have such great joy in knowing that the God of the universe knows us personally and loves us lavishly. To give lavishly means to give without limit. First John 3:1 (NIV) says, "See what great love the Father has lavished on us, that we should be called children of God! And that is what we are!" If you remember nothing else about God, remember this: He loves you without limit! Remember this as you start your day and eat your breakfast. Thank Him for His love and share His love with everyone you see today with a smile or a kind word. God says, *"I love you!"* Can you hear Him?

God, thank You for Your lavish love. I can't begin to understand how You can know everything about me and still love me without limit! I love You, God. I love You so much!

The Trap

I have learned to be happy with whatever I have.
PHILIPPIANS 4:11

Girls often compare themselves to each other. Who has the longest hair? Who has the cutest shoes? Who has the best toys or games? But that's not what God wants us to do. Do you want to know why? Because comparison is a thief. It steals your joy away. Can you think of a time when this happened? Maybe you got a pair of sparkly new tennis shoes for your birthday. But then you wore them to school and saw someone with shoes you or someone else thought were cuter. Suddenly your shoes didn't seem so sparkly anymore, and maybe you even felt a little sad. Do you see the trap? It matters to God that you're happy with what you have instead of wishing for what your friends have. This can be hard, but you can always ask Him for help.

Lord, please help me be content with what I have. I'm thankful for everything You've blessed me with.

Always with You, Always Working

The Lord will finish the work He started for me.
O Lord, Your loving-kindness lasts forever.
Do not turn away from the works of Your hands.
PSALM 138:8

God is with you always. You are His princess, and He promises to never leave you. You are a daughter of the King, and He has wonderful plans for your life. God is also always working on your behalf, and He will even miraculously turn painful things into good things as you trust in Him! Check out Romans 8:28 (NIV): "And we know that in all things God works for the good of those who love him, who have been called according to his purpose." As you grow up, you'll have lots of distractions in life trying to get you to turn away from trusting in God's great love for you. That's our enemy's main purpose. So remember how much God loves you and hide Psalm 138:8 in your heart.

God, thank You for never leaving
me alone. I love You, Lord.

Friends with God

The Lord spoke to Moses face to face, as a man speaks to his friend. When Moses returned to the other tents, his servant Joshua, the son of Nun, a young man, would not leave the meeting tent.

Exodus 33:11

The Bible tells us God spoke to Moses just like a friend. A face-to-face friendship with God is not to be taken lightly. It wasn't even possible for most people back in Moses' time. But now God has chosen *you* to be His friend! Remember John 15:15? Jesus said, "I have called you friends, for everything that I learned from my Father I have made known to you" (NIV). What feelings does this stir up in your heart? As you pray, talk to God just like you would talk to your friends. Do you ever write your friends notes? Write a note to God as your prayer today.

God, it's really amazing that You call me Your friend because of Jesus. Thank You for making a way for us to be friends. Help me never forget what You've done.

New Every Morning

It is because of the Lord's loving-kindness that we are not destroyed for His loving-pity never ends. It is new every morning. He is so very faithful.
LAMENTATIONS 3:22–23

God's love never ends, and neither does His mercy. Do you know what His mercy means? It means He doesn't punish us for our sins like we deserve. He does this because of what Jesus did for us on the cross. The Bible says God's mercies are new every morning. So if you feel like you've made a bunch of mistakes today, talk to God about them. Ask Him to forgive you and give you a pure heart. Then go to sleep in peace knowing that our great God forgives you and loves you. He is always ready to give you a fresh start each morning.

God, thank You for a fresh start and for forgiving my sins. Thank You for Your mercy and love that never ends. Help me follow You with my whole heart today.

The Lost Son

"While he was yet a long way off, his father saw him. The father was full of loving-pity for him. He ran and threw his arms around him and kissed him."

Luke 15:20

Jesus told a story about a son who left home and spent all his inheritance money on really dumb things. He was hungry and had nothing left to do but go crawling back to his dad and beg for forgiveness. He thought his dad was going to be really mad at him. But Jesus said the father was full of love and compassion for him. He was watching for his son to return, and he ran out to meet him while he was still a long way off. Jesus told us this story to show how God feels about us when we come to Him. We matter to Him so much that He waits patiently for us, and then He blesses us with His love.

Jesus, thank You for loving me so much, even when I've made mistakes.

Forgiveness Matters

"Watch yourselves! If your brother sins, speak sharp words to him. If he is sorry and turns from his sin, forgive him. What if he sins against you seven times in one day? If he comes to you and says he is sorry and turns from his sin, forgive him."
Luke 17:3–4

Jesus wants us to be quick to forgive. When we carry unforgiveness in our hearts, it gets really heavy. That's called bitterness. And when we hang on to bitterness, it can mess up all our other relationships too. You're too important to God to carry bitterness around. So how can you be quick to forgive? As soon as something happens that hurts you, take it straight to Jesus. Tell Him how you feel and ask Him to give you His thoughts about it. He will help you feel His supernatural love for the person who hurt you. Then you can let what happened go and ask Jesus for wisdom about what to say and do.

Jesus, please help me see other people through Your eyes and forgive them quickly.

You’ve Got the Joy

“But now I come to You, Father. I say these things while I am in the world. In this way, My followers may have My joy in their hearts.”

John 17:13

Your feelings and your attitude matter to Jesus. And guess what? Jesus promises to fill you with His joy just by spending time with Him. Psalm 16:11 (NIV) says, “You make known to me the path of life; you will fill me with joy in your presence.” Spend time with Jesus, and He’ll fill you with joy. How cool is that! Jesus is with you in this very moment. If you’re having trouble feeling joy, get alone somewhere and just talk to God. Tell Him exactly how you feel, either out loud, in your mind, or by jotting it in a journal. Jesus wants you to have joy in your heart. And if you don’t, He will help!

Jesus, I’m thankful for Your promise of joy as I spend time with You. Help me know and experience Your true joy.

Guaranteed Reservation

"There are many rooms in My Father's house. If it were not so, I would have told you. I am going away to make a place for you. After I go and make a place for you, I will come back and take you with Me. Then you may be where I am."

John 14:2–3

Think about the house you live in. How many rooms does it have? If you invited everyone from your school and church to come over, would they all fit inside? Probably not. We don't know everything about what heaven will be like because the Bible doesn't give us a ton of details, but we do know God's house is not like our houses. Heaven has plenty of space for everyone who loves Jesus. Jesus says you matter. He says He wants you to be with Him forever and that He's preparing a special place just for you!

Jesus, I'm so excited to have a reservation in Your house for all eternity! Thanks for making a place for me.

Always a Way Out

You have never been tempted to sin in any different way than other people. God is faithful. He will not allow you to be tempted more than you can take. But when you are tempted, He will make a way for you to keep from falling into sin.

1 Corinthians 10:13

The Bible tells us our enemy, Satan, is the father of lies and that he will try every trick in the book to get you to mess up. What did Jesus do when He was tempted? He told Satan the truth from God's Word. When you feel like you're being tempted to make a bad choice, ask Jesus for help. He's been there! He knows how to help you overcome. It matters to Jesus that you know there is always a way out of sin. He can help you make the right choice in the moment. And when you memorize scripture, God will help you remember those powerful words right when you need them. Start with 1 Corinthians 10:13!

Jesus, when I'm tempted,
help me remember Your truth.

Don't Judge. Smile!

"Do not say what is wrong in other people's lives. Then other people will not say what is wrong in your life."
MATTHEW 7:1

Judging people happens in so many TV shows, from how well someone sings to how well they bake a cake or wear their makeup. Our society is trained to judge people. But to be like Jesus, we need to stop judging other people. We need to love them for who they are, not for what they look like or how well they sing. The next time you meet someone new, be kind. That person matters to Jesus too. Give them a smile and get to know them for who they are and for the gifts God gave them. Look past how they look to see the amazing person God created. Only God is the judge of people's hearts, motives, and actions. You just be you!

Jesus, forgive me for the times I've judged people without getting to know who they really are. Please allow me to see others as You see them.

A Strong Foundation Matters

"Whoever hears these words of Mine and does them, will be like a wise man who built his house on rock. The rain came down. The water came up. The wind blew and hit the house. The house did not fall because it was built on rock."
MATTHEW 7:24–25

Have you ever gone to the beach and seen a house built right on the sand? That's scary! If a big storm comes, a house can fall apart and wash away if it doesn't have a stable foundation. Jesus tells this story about a house to teach us about life as a Christian. If we build our lives on the firm foundation of Jesus, we won't fall apart when hard things happen. We trust in God! But if we don't have a solid foundation in Jesus, we *can* fall apart when hard things happen. Put your trust in the solid rock of Jesus. He will never let you fall!

Jesus, I know You are my strong foundation that will be with me no matter what storms and troubles come my way.

Jesus, My Teacher

"All your sons will be taught by the Lord,
and the well-being of your children will be great."
Isaiah 54:13

You probably know a lot of teachers. They know a lot too, yet they don't know everything. But imagine being taught by someone who created all things and really does know the answer to every question! Jesus wants to be your teacher. If you've accepted Him as your Savior, His Spirit is alive in you, teaching you all things. Jesus has all authority and power over everything! Why is this important for you? It means you can go to Jesus with all your questions. It means He has authority over everything that comes and will come your way in this life. It means He's bigger than all your problems, failures, and fears. And you have access to this power at every moment!

I'm so thankful that You have authority over everything, Jesus, including my life! I ask You to teach me and lead me as I live this life You've given me.

Wind and Waves

They said, "What kind of a man is He?
Even the winds and the waves obey Him."
MATTHEW 8:27

Have you ever been outside when a rainstorm came on suddenly? That can be a scary experience! Wind and lightning can do great damage. The Bible tells us about a big storm that appeared while Jesus and His disciples were on a boat. Jesus was asleep, and when the waves were sweeping up over the sides of the boat, the disciples thought they were going to drown! They woke up Jesus, begging for His help. The good thing is that they went to the right person! Jesus told the wind and waves to stop, and they did! Isn't that amazing? Jesus still holds the same power over all of nature today. That means you can always ask Him for help. When you're tempted to doubt God's power and love for you, remember that the winds and the waves still obey Him!

Lord, please give me the
faith to believe in Your power.

Your Thoughts Matter

Jesus knew what they were thinking. He said, "Why do you think bad thoughts in your hearts?"

Matthew 9:4

Some people were judging Jesus, and He knew what they were thinking and called them out on it. Another Bible translation says Jesus asked them, "Why do you entertain evil thoughts in your hearts?" (NIV). The thing is, we can choose what we think about. "Entertaining a thought" means you think about it a lot and you won't stop yourself from thinking about it—so much so that it starts to affect your behavior. That's why your thoughts matter to Jesus. Second Corinthians 10:5 tells us to take hold of every thought and make them obey Him. So how do you do that? When you have a bad or scary thought, take it directly to Jesus. Ask Him to take the bad or scary thought away. Then ask Jesus to fill your mind with something that comes from Him.

Jesus, please help me entertain good thoughts that honor You.

A Friend to Everyone

Jesus heard them and said, "People who are well do not need a doctor. But go and understand these words, 'I want loving-kindness and not a gift to be given.' For I have not come to call good people. I have come to call those who are sinners."

MATTHEW 9:12–13

Jesus did many things to show that everyone mattered to Him. One thing He did made a lot of people mad. He had dinner with some people who were considered pretty sinful. But Jesus was a friend of sinners. He had the healing and the answers sinful people needed to change their lives, and many followed Him because He was willing to be a friend to everyone. Jesus still has the answers for our sinful world. Pray for the people around you who need Jesus and ask Him for opportunities to share God's love with them.

Jesus, please fill me with loving-kindness for the people around me–even the ones who are hard to love. Help me be a friend to everyone who needs You.

Your Father's Angels

"Be sure you do not hate one of these little children. I tell you, they have angels who are always looking into the face of My Father in heaven."

MATTHEW 18:10

You matter so much to God that He sends His angels to watch over you. When I was a little girl, I was lost in a "haunted house" at an amusement park. The haunted house was scary, and I was all alone. Then a tall, bright-looking man took my hand and led me to the exit where I soon found my family. The man disappeared after that. Was he an angel? I won't know for sure until I get to heaven, but I like to believe he was. We aren't supposed to worship or pray to angels, but they are God's messengers and warriors. God has special plans for your life, and He sends His angels to guard and protect you so those plans can happen.

Jesus, thank You for sending Your angels to guard and protect me! I feel so safe knowing that You love me in this way.

The Friends of Jesus

Jesus called His twelve followers to Him.
He gave them power to put out demons and to
heal all kinds of sickness and disease.
MATTHEW 10:1

Jesus asked twelve ordinary guys to follow Him. They were mostly fishermen, and they probably thought they could never be used by God. Jesus wasn't mean and bossy when He asked them. He gave them each a choice, and they became His friends. Then through these everyday, regular guys, God changed the world. Jesus gave them power to heal sickness and cast out demons. He used them to show that God can use anyone! The same is true today. You may not think you have any great talents or gifts God can use. But God can use anything you bring to Him and turn it into something that brings honor to Him and blessing to you. If you're a friend of Jesus', He has great plans for you!

Jesus, I trust Your great plans for me. I bring all that I have to You to use. Thanks for being my friend.

Family Matters

God makes a home for those who are alone.
PSALM 68:6

Family matters to Jesus. God doesn't want us to be lonely, so He made us to be in a community with other people. We learn from one another, and we grow and share God's love when we live in relationship with other people. You are a child of God, so that means you're part of God's family! That also means other Christians all over the world are your brothers and sisters in Christ. Being part of the family of God means you can share with your fellow believers and that you can encourage one another. If you're having a hard time finding good friends right now, ask Jesus for help! He cares about your relationships and wants you to have the family of God around you to help you.

Jesus, will You help me find other believers who love You and want to follow You? Please show me what it means to be a part of Your family.

Never Afraid

When the followers heard this, they got down on the ground on their faces and were very much afraid. Jesus came and put His hand on them. He said, "Get up! Do not be afraid."

Matthew 17:6–7

Jesus was with His friends when something made them really scared. Jesus knew they were afraid, so He touched them and told them they had nothing to be afraid of. Jesus is so caring! When you're with Him, you have no reason to be afraid. You can trust Him completely. Why? Because everything Jesus does is out of love for you. He never lies, and He always keeps His promises. He can turn any bad situation around and use it for good. That's why you don't have to be afraid when things become a little scary. Jesus is with you, and you can trust Him to lovingly care for you.

Thank You that I never have to be afraid when I'm with You, Jesus. And I know You're with me always!

God's Purpose for You

Jesus said to him, " 'You must love the Lord your God with all your heart and with all your soul and with all your mind.' This is the first and greatest of the Laws. The second is like it, 'You must love your neighbor as you love yourself.' "

MATTHEW 22:37–39

What are you supposed to do with your life? Get good grades in school? Go on to college? Start a family? That's what most people in this country consider their purpose, also known as "the American dream." Those are all nice goals, but is that really all God wants from us as His followers? Read 1 Corinthians 13:1–3. What does that passage tell you about all those plans? You could achieve the American dream and so much more, but it would all count for nothing if you didn't do it out of love for Jesus and others. God's purpose for us might not always be easy, but it is simple: love Him and love others.

Jesus, please change my heart
to match Your purpose for my life.

Upside Down

"The person who is not trying to honor himself will be made important."
Matthew 23:12

Have you noticed the upside-down theme in Jesus' words, that His ideas seem different from what the world thinks? He says we love others by serving them. He says the first shall be last and the last shall be first. He says the humble person will be lifted up. He says being great comes from serving others. These ideas are completely upside down from what our world believes. Many kids today (and adults!) focus on how many likes they can get on their YouTube videos. They're upset when they don't get enough attention on their social media posts. But Jesus says the person who's not trying to get the most attention will be made important. If you spend your life in the service of Jesus and others, you'll find that your heart overflows with joy—and it won't matter how many likes you get from people you don't even know!

Jesus, help me embrace Your upside-down world and find joy in serving others.

The Needy Matter

"For I was hungry and you gave Me food to eat.
I was thirsty and you gave Me water to drink.
I was a stranger and you gave Me a room."
Matthew 25:35

Did you know that when we serve others we're serving Jesus? In Matthew 25:40 (NIV), Jesus says, "Truly I tell you, whatever you did for one of the least of these brothers and sisters of mine, you did for me." When you see someone in need, can you picture Jesus being the one in need instead? Think of families at Christmastime who don't have money to buy gifts. What if it was Jesus who had no gifts? Could you find a way to help? Sit down with your family and think about ways you can get involved with needy people in your community. Find out how you can help—and remember that you're serving Jesus as you do it!

Jesus, I want to help take care of needs in
my community. Thank You for Your blessings!
Help me share these blessings with those in need.

The Fear Rescue

Jesus healed those who were sick of many kinds of diseases. He put out many demons. Jesus would not allow the demons to speak because they knew Who He was.

Mark 1:34

Your fears matter to God. Whether you have a bad dream or face a scary basement, He cares about you. Here are two scripture verses that can help:

- "At the name of Jesus every knee should bow, in heaven and on earth and under the earth." Philippians 2:10 NIV
- "The Spirit who lives in you is greater than the spirit who lives in the world." 1 John 4:4 NLT

Jesus' Spirit is alive in you, and that's bigger than anything scary. His name also has great power. Whenever you feel afraid, say the name of Jesus out loud. Sometimes that's the best prayer you can pray. When you call on Jesus' name, you're asking Him to take your fears and fill you with His love. Darkness leaves when Jesus enters.

Jesus, I trust that there is power in Your name. Thank You for rescuing me from fear.

In Jesus' Name

"You see and know this man here. He has been made strong through faith in Jesus' name. Yes, it is faith in Christ that has made this man well and strong."

Acts 3:16

In the book of Acts, Peter and John were telling their listeners all about what Jesus had done and the power available to those who believed. Peter even healed a crippled man who then jumped to his feet and began praising God. The crippled man was healed through faith in the name of Jesus. Jesus' name is not to be used lightly. It's not a magic word, and it should never be used in vain (that means don't use His name as a cussword). There is power in the name of Jesus because Jesus Himself gives the power. You can say the name of Jesus out loud as a prayer anytime. Just remember that it's Jesus hearing you call His name. He's the one with the power.

Jesus, help me honor Your name and have faith in the power of what You can do.

God's Kingdom

Jesus said to them, "The holy nation of God is not coming in such a way that can be seen with the eyes. It will not be said, 'See, here it is!' or, 'There it is!' For the holy nation of God is in you."
Luke 17:20–21

When you invite Jesus into your heart and choose to follow Him, the kingdom of God begins at that moment in your heart. Yes, we're waiting for Jesus to return so we can physically be with Him for eternity. And yes, one day Jesus will make all things new and destroy all evil forever. But we don't have to wait for heaven to be a part of God's kingdom. It's already begun! Jesus wants us to experience full and joyful lives (John 10:10) right here on earth. He wants to fill us with His light and love so other people will want to be filled with His light and love too.

Jesus, I'm so thankful we're friends and that I get to experience Your love and joy both now and for all eternity!

Alive in You

"I have made Your name known to them and will make it known. So then the love You have for Me may be in them and I may be in them."

JOHN 17:26

Did you know that Jesus prays for you? In John 17, He prayed that the same love God the Father has for His Son, Jesus, would be inside you. Isn't that awesome? When Jesus was here on earth, He had limits because He was in a human body. He couldn't be everywhere at the same time. Now that He has risen and conquered death, His Spirit can be everywhere at once. The Bible tells us, "God decided to let his people know this rich and glorious truth which he has for all people. This truth is Christ himself, who is in you. He is our only hope for glory" (Colossians 1:27 ICB). Having Jesus alive inside us is our only hope, now and forever.

Jesus, thank You for praying for me.
I'm so glad You're alive in me!

Obeying God Matters

"We must obey God instead of men!"
Acts 5:29

Sometimes when people start feeling big to you, God might start feeling small. Grown-ups, teachers, and friends might all be telling you to do something, and their being happy with you might seem pretty important because you want them to like you. But it's much more important to please Jesus than it is to please a person, and you know in your heart that Jesus wants you to do something else. Ask God to give you the strength to say the right thing at the right time and to do what He's asking you to do. If God feels too small to you and people seem too big, tell Jesus how you feel. Jesus gave His disciples courage and power through His Spirit. They were able to stand up for their faith even under severe attack. He will help you too.

Jesus, sometimes I'm confused. I need
Your help to know what to say and do.
I want to please You, not just other people.

Christ's Spirit

God says, "In the last days I will send My Spirit on all men. Then your sons and daughters will speak God's Word."
Acts 2:17

God knew we couldn't figure out life alone. He knew we would need a helper to teach us and lead us. So He sent His very own Spirit to live and grow inside us. This is so important, which is why we talk about it over and over! Listen to this: "Spiritually alive, we have access to everything God's Spirit is doing. . . . Isaiah's question, 'Is there anyone around who knows God's Spirit, anyone who knows what he is doing?' has been answered: Christ knows, and we have Christ's Spirit" (1 Corinthians 2:15–16 MSG). When we have the Spirit of Jesus alive in us, we're being transformed, God's Word is brought to life in us, and we're taught right and wrong. Because you matter so much to Jesus, He sent His Spirit to come alive in you.

Jesus, I'm happy that You sent me Your Spirit to teach me and to help me follow You.

The Ministry of Jesus

"The Holy Spirit was promised by the Father. God has given Him to us. That is what you are seeing and hearing now!"
ACTS 2:33

In her book *Tramp for the Lord*, author Corrie ten Boom wrote, "When you are filled with the Holy Spirit, then the ministry of Jesus just flows out of you." Jesus promised to send us the Holy Spirit, and He did. But we have to accept the help of God's Spirit. God wants us to be filled with His Spirit to remind us of everything Jesus said and to remind us how loved we are and how much we matter to Him. He will help us hear from God. He will give us wisdom and lead us in the right direction. Jesus has special things for you to do. Allow Him to fill you with His Spirit so His ministry will flow out of you too.

Jesus, I don't want to just work for You without Your help. Please fill me with Your Spirit.

You're Important

He took the children in His arms. He put His hands on them and prayed that good would come to them.

Mark 10:16

Back in Bible times, women and children weren't considered important. They were even treated as property sometimes. Isn't that sad? This was not God's plan for women or children! Jesus came to show another way. He loved and respected women and children and spent lots of time with them. Jesus was offended when the disciples tried to keep children away from Him. He stood up for children and told the disciples not to prevent kids from coming. He honored women and children and made them feel important. He said, "Anyone who will not receive the kingdom of God like a little child will never enter it" (Mark 10:15 NIV). The faith of children is pure and strong. They believe someone who feels safe to them. Jesus wants all His children, old and young, to have faith like that!

I'm so thankful that I'm important to You, Jesus. Help me keep my faith strong and pure.

Sharing Matters

The many followers acted and thought the same way. None of them said that any of their things were their own, but they shared all things.
Acts 4:32

The Bible tells us no one in the early church was needy. If someone was sick or needed food or had a need of any kind, the other Christians sold their possessions to help. They didn't consider anything they owned to be off-limits, and they realized that everything they had was a gift from God. God blessed them even more for that. How do you feel about your stuff? Do you realize that everything you have is a gift and a blessing from God? Sharing shows that you know everyone matters to God. Is there a way you could bless someone in your community who doesn't have as much as you have? Get together with your family and discuss ways you can help with needs in your community.

Jesus, please open opportunities for my family to share what we have with other people, because they matter to You too.

Doubt

Jesus said to him, "Thomas, because you have seen Me, you believe. Those are happy who have never seen Me and yet believe!"
JOHN 20:29

Thomas was one of Jesus' disciples, who doubted that Jesus had risen from the dead even after witnessing Jesus' many miracles firsthand! Grown-ups have a hard time believing in miracles sometimes. Do you? Sometimes we wish we could see Jesus face-to-face just like Thomas did. But did you catch what Jesus said? "Those are happy who have never seen Me and yet believe!" Jesus was talking about you and me! He said we're happy and blessed because we have faith without actually seeing Jesus with our own eyes. What do you think He meant? The Message paraphrase of John 20:29 helps us understand a bit more: "Jesus said, 'So, you believe because you've seen with your own eyes. Even better blessings are in store for those who believe without seeing.'" When you're tempted to doubt, remember the truth from God's Word.

Jesus, help me believe even though I can't see. Chase away my doubt with Your truth.

Your Prayers

"Pray like this: 'Our Father in heaven, Your name is holy. May Your holy nation come. What You want done, may it be done on earth as it is in heaven. Give us the bread we need today. Forgive us our sins as we forgive those who sin against us. Do not let us be tempted, but keep us from sin. Your nation is holy. You have power and shining-greatness forever. Let it be so.' "

MATTHEW 6:9–13

Jesus gave us a good example for how to pray. You can add whatever else you'd like to your prayers, but the important thing is to simply pray to Jesus and tell Him what's on your heart. He already knows everything about you, but He loves it when you talk to Him. Try picturing Jesus in your mind while you pray. God loves to use our imaginations as we talk to Him. After all, He created them!

Jesus, thank You for showing me how to be more like You. Thank You for giving me a great imagination. Please use it as I pray.

Time with Jesus Matters

They were surprised and wondered how easy it was for Peter and John to speak. They could tell they were men who had not gone to school. But they knew they had been with Jesus.

ACTS 4:13

Peter and John were two of Jesus' followers who were obeying His command to go tell the world about Him. They weren't educated men. They were just regular guys. But they were courageous because they knew Jesus personally. The people knew by their words and actions that they must have been given supernatural power (special power from God), and they could tell that Peter and John had been with Jesus! Do you think people can tell when you've been with Jesus? Why or why not? Does your time with Jesus change the way you act and the way you love other people? Does Jesus make you more courageous?

Jesus, I really do want people to be able to tell that I've spent time with You. Please use our time together to change my thoughts and actions to match Yours.

God's Word Is True

Jesus did many other powerful works in front of His followers. They are not written in this book. But these are written so you may believe that Jesus is the Christ, the Son of God.

John 20:30–31

As followers of Jesus, we trust that the Bible is the inspired Word of God. What does the word *inspired* mean? It means God supernaturally helped the Bible to be written. Lots of scriptures in the Bible tell us about this. How else can we know the Bible is true? On AnswersInGenesis.org, Dr. Jason Lisle says this about the Bible: "It has been confirmed countless times by archaeology and other sciences. It possesses divine insight into the nature of the universe and has made correct predictions about distant future events with perfect accuracy." The Word of God can be trusted. When you're tempted to doubt the truth of God's Word, ask Jesus to speak to you through it. See what happens!

Jesus, thank You that I can know for sure that Your Word is true!

Jesus Shows Up

After He had suffered much and then died, He showed Himself alive in many sure ways for forty days.

Acts 1:3

A former atheist (someone who doesn't believe God is real) came to our church and shared how he found Jesus when he was trying to prove that He didn't exist. Isn't that amazing? He found that it would take more faith on his part to keep believing that there is no God than to accept the facts of history that Jesus was (and is) real, that He was (and is) God, and that He rose from the dead! Not only is the Bible the inspired Word of God, but it's a reliable historical textbook proven true throughout the centuries. You may have doubts about your faith sometimes, but Jesus understands. Ask Him to show you how real He is. You'll be amazed at the way He shows up in your life!

Jesus, I want to believe You and trust You with my life. Please help me see You in my world.

Jesus and Mama Chicks

"How many times I wanted to gather your children around Me, as a chicken gathers her young ones under her wings. But you would not let Me."
MATTHEW 23:37

Jesus says He wants to comfort His followers just like a mama chicken gathers her babies close to her wings to protect them from harm and lead them in the right direction. Can you picture Jesus doing that for you when you're sad? Go ahead and give it a try! Jesus created your imagination, and He wants to use it for His glory. Ask Jesus to show you a picture of Him comforting you! Can you see Jesus in your imagination? What is He doing? Draw a picture of what Jesus showed you so you'll always remember that He is with you. Write Matthew 23:37 on your picture and hang it on your wall.

Jesus, thank You for using my imagination to speak to me. It makes me so happy that You want to comfort me and love me like a mama loves her chicks.

Chosen

Jesus said to them, "Have you not read in the Holy Writings, 'The Stone that was put aside by the workmen has become the most important Stone in the building? The Lord has done this. We think it is great!' "

Matthew 21:42

Have you ever felt forgotten or left out? Jesus knows exactly what this feels like. God's Word tells us Jesus had some friends and followers, but most people not only rejected Him but sent Him to die on a cross. They humiliated Him. It's hard to imagine how difficult this must have been for Jesus, but He endured it all out of His deep love for us. Men rejected Jesus, but God had chosen Him. Remember this the next time you feel alone or forgotten. God chose you to be His much-loved daughter. Jesus sees everything happening to you, and He understands your heart. He is with you. You are never alone.

Jesus, help me remember that You know exactly how I feel. Thanks for choosing me and understanding me.

The Last Are First

"Many who are first will be last.
Many who are last will be first."
MATTHEW 19:30

It's fun to play follow the leader when you get to go first and everyone else follows. The problems come when you want to be first at everything, all the time. So many kids and grown-ups have never outgrown "me first" thinking. These people end up with broken relationships with God and people. Jesus showed us another way. He put other people first, and He served them. Jesus tells us that in the kingdom of heaven, the first will be last and the last will be first. Jesus also tells us that it doesn't matter if you're rich or you're poor, famous or unknown. Those things don't get you into heaven any faster. In God's kingdom, we matter simply because of Jesus' love for us!

Jesus, forgive me when I'm selfish and want to be first at everything. Help me have love for others and put them first. Thank You that I matter simply because You love me.

Praying Together Matters

"For where two or three are gathered together in My name, there I am with them."
MATTHEW 18:20

Jesus says something powerful happens when believers pray together. Sometimes it might feel weird to pray out loud in front of other people, but your prayers together are powerful! The Message paraphrase of Matthew 18:20 says it this way: "When two of you get together on anything at all on earth and make a prayer of it, my Father in heaven goes into action. And when two or three of you are together because of me, you can be sure that I'll be there." When we pray with other people who also have the Holy Spirit living inside them, asking Jesus to make His plans and ideas happen, amazing things do happen! Tonight at bedtime, take turns talking to God with a parent or another family member. Ask for God's will to be done in a specific situation that affects your family.

Jesus, thank You for being with us in powerful ways when we pray together.

A Little Girl and Jesus

While Jesus talked to them, a leader of the people came and got down before Him, and worshiped Him. He said, "My daughter has just died. But come, lay Your hand on her and she will live."
Matthew 9:18

A little girl died, and a crowd of people laughed at Jesus in unbelief when He came to her house to help her. After all, she was dead! What could He do? But the girl's father believed. He went to Jesus and asked for help, and Jesus said He would. Jesus took the girl by her hand, and she got up! To the crowd, this situation seemed hopeless. But the father trusted that Jesus was who He said He was. Jesus loves children, and you are so important to Him! Your faith in the God of miracles will make all the difference in your life. Jesus can do anything! He takes hold of your hand. You matter to Him!

Jesus, thank You for holding my hand and loving me. I trust You to do the impossible. I love You, Jesus!

Everyone Matters

A man with a bad skin disease came and got down before Him and worshiped Him. He said, "Lord, if You will, You can heal me!" Then Jesus put His hand on him and said, "I will. You are healed!" At once the man was healed.

MATTHEW 8:2–3

Back in Bible times, leprosy was a scary skin disease because it had no cure. People were also afraid of catching it. If someone got leprosy, they were banished from their homes and sent to live with other sick people called lepers. No one wanted to even touch someone with this disease. But Jesus did! He touched the leper we're told about in Matthew 8, which shows that everyone matters to Jesus! How can you have more compassion for people? Talk about some ideas with your family. Ask Jesus for opportunities to show His love through compassion. Compassionate people show that everyone matters to Jesus.

Jesus, please help me see people who are in need and give me wisdom to know how to help them. I want to be a compassionate person.

God Gives You His Strength

He gives strength to the weak. And He gives power to him who has little strength.
Isaiah 40:29

Growing up will be a great adventure. And like any adventure, both good things and hard things will make it interesting. If you focus only on all the hard things this life brings you, though, it's easy to have big feelings that seem overwhelming or too much. But you matter so much to God that He gives you His very own strength! He's placed His own Spirit right inside you, giving you all the strength you could ever need to get through anything. You don't have to get the power from yourself. God is all-powerful, and because you're His beloved daughter, you have access to that power in every single moment. How amazing is that? Make sure you're tapping into that power when you feel like life is too much.

Lord, I'm amazed at the truth that Your power lives inside me. Thank You that I don't have to figure things out on my own.

Deep Water

"Do not let your heart be troubled. You have put your trust in God, put your trust in Me also."
JOHN 14:1

Jesus wants you to trust Him and not be afraid. He is good, and He loves you so much. Check out Psalm 18:16 and 19 (NLT): "He reached down from heaven and rescued me; he drew me out of deep waters. . . . He led me to a place of safety; he rescued me because he delights in me." "Deep waters" in verse 16 is another way of saying "hard times" or "troubles." Maybe some kids at school are mean. Maybe you have a friend or family member who's sick. Maybe your dog passed away. All that matters to Jesus, and He wants to reach down from heaven and support you. The Bible says He will lead you to a place of safety. He can send people and supplies to meet any need you have. Just talk to Him about it. Jesus loves to show you what He can do.

Jesus, I trust that You can rescue me from any troubles.

Open Arms

"All whom My Father has given to Me will come to Me.
I will never turn away anyone who comes to Me."
JOHN 6:37

Whether you go to Jesus for the first time or the millionth time, you can be sure His arms are open. He'll always run to meet you. And that's even if you've messed up. Romans 2:4 tells us that the kindness of God leads us to Jesus to have our sins forgiven, and in John 6:37 Jesus says He'll never turn away anyone who comes to Him. If you've made a big mistake, the best thing you can do is go straight to Jesus and talk to Him about it. He won't make you feel shame or make you feel bad about yourself. Instead, He'll tell you He loves you and show you ways you can change.

Jesus, I'm so thankful that You remind me how much You love me and that You'll never turn me away when I make mistakes. I know You're always ready to forgive me.

God Is Faithful

God has said, "I will never leave you or let you be alone."
HEBREWS 13:5

Remember what being faithful means? It means keeping promises and doing what you said you were going to do. But here's the thing: no one is completely faithful all the time. That is, except Jesus. Even the best parents forget to pack a kid's lunch now and again. People are human. They make mistakes and forget sometimes. But Jesus is faithful all the time! And He directs all His love and faithfulness right toward you. He will never forget you. He'll never give up on you. He'll never lie to you. He'll never, ever stop loving you. Nothing you could ever do will change His mind about how much He loves you. That's a big deal! The biggest! God looks at you and smiles because He sees Jesus in you. God is your loving parent who never gets it wrong.

Jesus, I'm thankful that I'm always on Your mind and that You always keep Your promises to me.

Deep Roots

Have your roots planted deep in Christ. Grow in Him. Get your strength from Him. Let Him make you strong in the faith as you have been taught. Your life should be full of thanks to Him.

Colossians 2:7

Have you ever seen a tree being cut down or dug out of the ground? Tree roots can be huge! The average tree roots are around twenty feet long, but some can be over a hundred feet long. Tree roots spread out wide. Trees are sturdy and strong when they have deep roots. God says He wants our faith in Christ to be deep like the roots of a tree. When our faith is strong, the winds of life can't blow us down. Your faith matters to God, and He wants you to stand strong in Him, just like a tree with deep roots.

God, I pray that You will grow my faith deep into the roots of Your love. I want to build my life on You and Your truth.

God Likes You

"This is life that lasts forever. It is to know You, the only true God, and to know Jesus Christ Whom You have sent."
John 17:3

So far, you've heard a lot about how much Jesus loves you. But do you think God *likes* you? Zephaniah 3:17 says, "The Lord your God is with you, a Powerful One Who wins the battle. He will have much joy over you. With His love He will give you new life. He will have joy over you with loud singing." When you come to know Jesus as your Savior, God washes away all your sins, and then He sees you as the perfect girl you really are. You can say with confidence, "Jesus likes me!" He rejoices over you and even sings about you! You are liked. You are loved. You are His!

God, thank You for loving me—and for liking me just the way I am. Thank You for seeing me as perfect. I love You. I like You a whole lot too.

The God of Miracles

Jesus said, "God can do things men cannot do."
LUKE 18:27

Do you know how great and powerful God is? Take a look at these verses:

- "Our Lord is great and very powerful. There is no limit to what he knows." Psalm 147:5 ICB
- "Do you realize where you are? You're in a cosmos star-flung with constellations by God, a world God wakes up each morning and puts to bed each night. God dips water from the ocean and gives the land a drink. GOD, God-revealed, does all this." Amos 5:8 MSG

God is the great Creator of all things, and yet He cares deeply about everything that matters to you! Jesus wants you to know how very loved you are. No matter what you're facing today, facing this year, or will face in the future, trust that God can do the impossible in your life. He is still the God of miracles.

Jesus, help my faith in You grow stronger. Help me believe that You can do anything!

Beauty from Inside

But the Lord said to Samuel, "Do not look at the way he looks on the outside or how tall he is, because I have not chosen him. For the Lord does not look at the things man looks at. A man looks at the outside of a person, but the Lord looks at the heart."

1 Samuel 16:7

The Bible says people look at outward appearance but God looks at the heart. You don't need the best hair or designer clothes to be precious to God. A truly beautiful person shines from the inside out. You are God's princess, and He created you just the way you are. Thank Him for your smile. Thank Him for making you with the special traits only you have. Ask God to give you a pure heart that will light up the rest of your body.

God, please create in me a beautiful and pure heart. Thanks for creating me just the way I am. Help me see myself as You see me.

Blessing Your Body

Do not let your beauty come from the outside. It should not be the way you comb your hair or the wearing of gold or the wearing of fine clothes. Your beauty should come from the inside. It should come from the heart. This is the kind that lasts. Your beauty should be a gentle and quiet spirit. In God's sight this is of great worth and no amount of money can buy it.

1 Peter 3:3–4

Do you ever wish you were created a little differently? Maybe with straighter hair or smoother skin? Maybe a little taller or shorter? Maybe without some real physical challenge you have? God wants you to know you're beautiful just the way you are! Get in front of a mirror, and then look at yourself up and down. Thank God for every part of your body, and ask Him to bless it with health and strength.

Lord, thank You for my body.
Help me accept myself just the way I am.

Everything You Do Matters

Whatever work you do, do it with all your heart. Do it for the Lord and not for men. Remember that you will get your reward from the Lord. He will give you what you should receive. You are working for the Lord Christ.

Colossians 3:23–24

Anything you do can be an act of worship to God. Everything you do matters to Him, and He sees you as you do your chores and homework. When you realize you're serving and worshipping God as you work, you become a joy to your family too. Ask God to help you with your chores and your homework. Ask Him to give you joy in serving your family and helping around the house. Turning worship music on while you work always helps too!

Lord, please help me work willingly at whatever I do, and help me remember that it's all about You and for You anyway! Help me to work hard at the tasks You've given me and to do the ones I don't enjoy with a good attitude.

God Is Bigger

There is no fear in love. Perfect love puts fear out of our hearts. People have fear when they are afraid of being punished. The man who is afraid does not have perfect love.

1 John 4:18

Lots of people are afraid of things, but some people live their whole lives in fear. You see these people at church, at school, or at the mall, but you might not know what they struggle with on the inside. They might even say they follow God, but their lives show more fear than faith. These people fear the future and anything unknown. But the Bible says we can live our lives without any fear! God's perfect love throws fear out of our hearts. Jesus wants us to come to Him with the faith of a child (Matthew 19:14), believing that God is bigger than anything we could ever face. Even in the scariest situation you could imagine, God is bigger!

God, thank You that You are with me and that I never have to be afraid.

The Open Door

"I say to you, ask, and what you ask for will be given to you. Look, and what you are looking for you will find. Knock, and the door you are knocking on will be opened to you. For everyone who asks, will receive what he asks for. Everyone who looks, will find what he is looking for. Everyone who knocks, will have the door opened to him."

Luke 11:9–10

Our questions, hopes, desires, needs, and worries matter to God, and He wants us to ask Him about anything. But a lot of times we forget to take things to God. James 4:2 (NIV) says, "You do not have because you do not ask God." We try to get our needs met by other people and with things when God is just waiting for us to come to Him for help. He wants to have a conversation with you when you both speak and you both listen. What do you need to talk to Him about today?

Lord, I'm thankful that Your door is always open to me.

Living in Love

We have come to know and believe the love God has for us. God is love. If you live in love, you live by the help of God and God lives in you.
1 John 4:16

John, one of Jesus' disciples, wrote the letter that became the book of 1 John to some of the first Christians. They were trying too hard to fit in with people who didn't know Jesus. Does that sound familiar? John and the other followers of Jesus had developed a close friendship with God through Jesus, and in this letter, John reminds them and us that this relationship is possible. Your relationship to God matters so much to Him! But what does that relationship look like? It's listening for God and getting to know His voice and then doing what He asks. Ask God to make Himself known to you. He will. . .if you're listening.

God, I want to love You with all my heart and soul. Lead me as I grow up knowing and following You.

Words Matter

"Whoever says to his brother, 'You have no brains,' will have to stand in front of the court."
MATTHEW 5:22

Chances are you've been upset with a friend or relative sometime, right? Maybe they were annoying you or not sharing the way you hoped they would. You might have even said something mean to them in the moment. Can you remember a time like that? This verse doesn't literally mean that you have to go to court if you tell your brother he's dumb. But Jesus is telling us that our words matter. They reveal what's really going on in our hearts. If you've hurt someone with your words, the best thing to do is talk to Jesus about it first and then go make it right with the person you hurt. Ask Jesus to give you His heart for your friend or relative.

Jesus, please help me be more careful with my words. Give me the courage to go to the person I've hurt and tell them I'm sorry.

Where You Go for Wisdom Matters

But the wisdom that comes from heaven is first of all pure. Then it gives peace. It is gentle and willing to obey. It is full of loving-kindness and of doing good. It has no doubts and does not pretend to be something it is not.

JAMES 3:17

These days, people go to Google or to some other internet search engine looking for wisdom. But the so-called wisdom they find might not be pure, peaceful, or good. Instead, it will be mixed with thousands of opinions so they'll have to sift through a bunch of junk to find some truth. So wisdom is rarely found online unless you're looking up God's Word! When you need wisdom, the Bible says you can ask God for it and He'll give it to you—just because you asked Him (James 1:5)! You never have to sift through any questionable content to find wisdom from God. He will give you pure answers that promote peace and love.

God, help me learn to come to You first when I need wisdom.

Everything You Need

He gives us everything we need for life and for holy living. He gives it through His great power. As we come to know Him better, we learn that He called us to share His own shining-greatness and perfect life.
2 Peter 1:3

God's Word says He has given us everything we need to live a life that honors Him. Did you catch that? He has given us *everything* we need! Everything God wants you to have and know right now is currently available to you. You don't have to wait until you go to church or finish school or get home from camp or grow up. You have everything you need to be close to God right now! You are free to be yourself and live the life God created you to live.

Jesus, I can't thank You enough for giving me everything I need to be close to You in each moment. Because of Your power, I am free to love You and be loved by You.

Neighbors Matter

"Which of these three do you think was a neighbor to the man who was beaten by the robbers?" The man who knew the Law said, "The one who showed loving-pity on him." Then Jesus said, "Go and do the same."

Luke 10:36–37

Jesus told a story about a good Samaritan. Do you remember what happened? Only one person stopped to help a man who had been beaten by robbers. All the other people walked right on by. The good Samaritan bandaged his wounds and took him to an inn to heal, even paying for his expenses. Our neighbors matter to Jesus, but who is your neighbor? Is it just your friends and the people you love? No, Jesus says anyone we come across is our neighbor. And He wants us to love our neighbors as ourselves. Sometimes that's difficult, especially if we have weird neighbors! But Jesus can help you love even the unlovable. Just ask Him!

Jesus, please help me love my neighbors in ways that bless You–even when it's hard.

Grace and Peace

God the Father was pleased to have everything made perfect by Christ, His Son. Everything in heaven and on earth can come to God because of Christ's death on the cross. Christ's blood has made peace.

Colossians 1:19–20

Remember, God wants you to see yourself the way He sees you. Do you remember how He sees you? If you need a refresher, go back to the lists on pages 16 and 17. Because of Jesus, God sees you as holy and blameless as you stand before Him—without a single fault! Can you believe it? God knows everything you've ever done, and He loves you anyway. You don't have to hide anything from God. You don't have to get all cleaned up before you go to Him either. Jesus is like the friend who shows up at your house and offers to help you clean up the big mess in your room. He helps you do the cleaning, every step of the way.

God, thank You for Your amazing grace for me!

Fear or Love?

We can come to God without fear because
we have put our trust in Christ.
Ephesians 3:12

What do you think of when you think of God? According to the Bible, the first thing we should think of is that God is love (check out 1 John 4:8). He loves you and wants the very best for you. Anything you hear about God that doesn't line up with that truth is a lie. God wants you to come to Him anytime about anything and everything. He cares about everything you care about. He wants you to be at peace and live a life of joy and love, even during hard times. He offers His presence in every moment. And His presence is what brings you joy and peace. Do you believe that? If you have trouble believing this is true, confess that to God. That just means talk to God about it and ask for help to believe His truth.

God, please help me believe
the truth about Your love.

The Best Choice

Jesus said to her, "Martha, Martha, you are worried and troubled about many things. Only a few things are important, even just one. Mary has chosen the good thing. It will not be taken away from her."

Luke 10:41–42

In the Bible, Martha was cooking and serving Jesus and His followers. Her sister Mary was sitting at Jesus' feet because she wanted to hear everything He had to say. Martha got mad at Mary for not helping and went to Jesus and told on her! But Jesus said Mary had made the better choice by choosing to be with Him instead of just doing work for Him. Have you ever volunteered to help at your church? Sometimes we get so distracted by the work we're doing *for* Jesus that we forget to take time to be *with* Him. Being with Jesus matters, not just doing work for Him.

Jesus, help me make the best choice like Mary did. I want to serve You well, but I need to spend more time with You.

You're a Missionary!

We are Christ's missionaries. God is speaking to you through us. We are speaking for Christ and we ask you from our hearts to turn from your sins and come to God.

2 Corinthians 5:20

The Holy Spirit works in us to carry out God's plans. In Ephesians 1:19–20 (NLT), the Christ follower Paul said, "I also pray that you will understand the incredible greatness of God's power for us who believe him. This is the same mighty power that raised Christ from the dead and seated him in the place of honor at God's right hand in the heavenly realms." Remember, this power is what is alive and working inside you today! Before Jesus returned to heaven, He told His followers to go into the world and tell everyone about the truth of Jesus and His kingdom. God has important things for you to do too! How can you begin telling everyone about the great power and love of Jesus?

Jesus, please fill my heart with Your love and courage as I tell people about Your great love for them.

Never Forget

I am sure that God Who began the good work in you will keep on working in you until the day Jesus Christ comes again.
Philippians 1:6

Here are some important reminders: God is with you always. He's listening, and He loves you as though you were the only girl in the universe! You are His child—a child of the King of all kings—and He will never abandon you. God has wonderful plans for your life. And you matter so much that, if you trust in Him, He'll miraculously turn even the painful things that happen into good things (Romans 8:28 again!). As you grow up, you'll have a lot of distractions trying to get you to doubt God's love for you and how much you matter. Never forget how much Jesus loves you! You can do this by hiding His Word in your heart (memorizing scripture) and asking the Holy Spirit to remind you of His truth whenever you start to doubt.

God, help me never forget
Your amazing love for me!

Last Words Matter

"Teach them to do all the things I have told you.
And I am with you always, even to the end of the world."
MATTHEW 28:20

After Jesus conquered death and rose from the grave, He appeared to His followers many times. The last thing He said to them and to us before He returned to heaven is this: "I am with you always." The last thing someone says to you is usually pretty important. And this is the most important thing God wanted us to know. He is Immanuel, God with us. Always. His Spirit is alive in our hearts. We matter to Him. Whenever you're tempted to doubt who God says you are, remember that He is with you. Ask Him to open your heart to believe how much you matter to Him.

Jesus, thank You for showing me how much I matter to You. When I'm tempted to doubt the truth and I'm feeling lousy, remind me who You are and who I am in You. Thank You for Your great love for me, Lord. I love You back.

Scripture Index

OLD TESTAMENT

NEW TESTAMENT